U0823519

pwc

普华永道

普华永道国际财务报告准则实务指引系列（第十三册）
PricewaterhouseCoopers IFRS MOA Series (Volume Thirteen)

Manual of Accounting — IFRS 2013

Chapter 33 – Service concession arrangements

国际财务报告准则实务指引

第三十三章——特许服务权安排

中英文对照

翻译组主要成员：谢智政　李宜桦　孙宇辉　陈骏业　黄志娜
陈贵鹏

中国财政经济出版社

This book has been prepared for general guidance on matters of interest only, and does not constitute professional advice. You should not act upon the information contained in this book without obtaining specific professional advice. No representation or warranty (express or implied) is given as to the accuracy or completeness of the information contained in this book, and, to the extent permitted by law, PricewaterhouseCoopers does not accept or assume any liability, responsibility or duty of care for any consequences of you or anyone else acting, or refraining to act, in reliance on the information contained in this book or for any decision based on it.

This book covers one of the chapters of the English version and its Chinese translation, which the English version remains the definitive source of guidance. The publishers and the authors cannot accept any responsibility for any errors or misunderstandings arising from the English version and its Chinese translation. Neither can the publishers and the authors accept any responsibility for loss occasioned to any person acting or refraining from action as a result of the material in this book.

Preface

Recent years have seen major changes in financial reporting worldwide with the single most important change being convergence around IFRS. There has also been a keen focus to improve the long term development of the CPA profession within China. As the Ministry of Finance and other regulatory bodies continue to promulgate legislation to promote the development of the Chinese CPA profession, we hope the release of our IFRS Manual of Accounting with Chinese Translation will also contribute to this effort.

The Ministry of Finance issued the Accounting Standards for Business Enterprises (hereafter referred to as "China Accounting Standards" or "CAS") in 2006. CAS incorporates all of the principles of IFRS and there has been a continued focus on convergence over the last few years. Additionally, IFRS is becoming increasingly important for many companies in China, including domestic companies seeking to raise capital overseas, as well as for foreign companies that have operations in China. With the continued convergence of CAS and IFRS, the release of our IFRS Manual of Accounting with Chinese Translation brings to China the extensive collective experience of the PwC's global network of firms in applying IFRS.

We hope this Manual will play a part in promoting consistent, comparable, relevant and reliable IFRS financial information and will serve as a reference tool for accounting students, academics, practitioners and users of financial statements in better understanding and implementing IFRS. More importantly, we hope the advice given in this text will assist those dealing with the many issues faced in preparing IFRS financial statements and provide helpful insight to users of such statements.

Raymund Chao
Asia Pacific Assurance Leader
PwC

前言

近年来，全球财务报告领域发生了重大变化，其中最为重要的一项变化是与国际财务报告准则的趋同。同时人们也热切地关注着中国境内注册会计师行业的长期发展。财政部及其他监管机构不断完善法规，推动中国注册会计师行业的发展，我们希望这本中英文对照的国际财务报告准则实务指引能够对此作出贡献。

财政部于2006年颁布了《企业会计准则》（以下称为中国会计准则，或CAS）。CAS包含了IFRS中的所有原则，且在过去的几年里持续趋同。此外，IFRS对于中国的许多公司来说越来越重要，包括寻求筹集海外资本的国内公司，以及在中国境内运营的外国公司。随着CAS与IFRS的持续趋同，本书的发行将给中国读者带来普华永道全球成员机构网络在应用IFRS方面积累的丰富的经验。

我们希望本书能够在推广一致的、可比的、相关的以及可靠的IFRS财务信息方面起到作用，并且可以作为会计领域的学生、学者、从业人员及财务报表使用者更好地理解及运用IFRS的参考工具。更为重要的是，我们希望本指引中提出的建议能够帮助其处理在编制IFRS财务报表时遇到的问题，并向此类财务报表使用者提供有用的观点。

赵柏基
普华永道亚太区审计部主管合伙人

Overview/Introduction

The IFRS Manual of Accounting is a practical guide to International Financial Reporting Standards. With close to 70 countries that have converged their local accounting standards with IFRS as at the time of writing, the application of IFRS has attracted significant attention in the world stage. At the same time, as more and more countries adopt IFRS (or its equivalent local standard), views continue to develop or evolve as to how particular aspects of a standard should be interpreted and applied. The views expressed in this Manual are based on years of experience from PricewaterhouseCoopers' Global Accounting Consulting Services team. The views expressed are a guide to applying IFRS rather than a set of definitive interpretations. The application of IFRS to a specific company is a matter of judgement given its particular facts and circumstances. Moreover, the application of IFRS might be influenced by the views of regulators.

The Manual covers diverse areas of accounting from the recognition and measurement of financial instruments to accounting for deferred taxation, business combinations and share-based payments. It explains in detail the rules that apply to preparing consolidated financial statements and considers the other statements that appear in annual reports such as cash flow statements as well as disclosures required by each specific standard.

Due to the continued convergence of China Accounting Standards and IFRS, PwC China has undertaken a significant project to translate our Global IFRS Manual of Accounting into Chinese. We sincerely hope that our IFRS Manual of Accounting with Chinese Translation provides practical insights to transactions commonly-seen in China and can help preparers, auditors, analysts and other users of financial statements to bridge the gap between accounting principles and their applications.

Yvonne Kam
Accounting Consulting Service Lead Partner
PwC China and Hong Kong

概述/引言

《国际财务报告准则实务指引》是应用国际财务报告准则的实务指南。于撰稿之时，已有近 70 个国家将其本国的会计准则与国际财务报告准则趋同，在世界范围内，国际财务报告准则的应用已广受重视。与此同时，随着越来越多的国家采用国际财务报告准则（或其等同的本地准则），关于某条准则特定方面应如何解释及应用的各种观点在持续发展或演变。本实务指引中所表达的观点是基于普华永道全球会计专业咨询服务团队以往多年的经验得出。我们所传达的观点是应用国际财务报告准则的指南，而非一系列确定的解释。一家特定的企业在应用国际财务报告准则时需根据特定的事实和环境作出判断。此外，国际财务报告准则的应用也可能受到监管机构观点的影响。

本实务指引涵盖从金融工具的确认和计量到递延税项、业务合并和以股份为基础的支付的核算等不同的会计领域。它详细解释了编制合并财务报表所应用的原则，并考虑了年报中出现的其他报表，如现金流量表以及每条特定准则所要求的披露。

鉴于中国会计准则与国际财务报告准则的持续趋同，普华永道中国启动了一项具有重大意义的项目，即将《国际财务报告准则实务指引》译成中文。我们诚挚地希望这套中英文对照的《国际财务报告准则实务指引》能够为中国常见的交易提供实用的见解，为编制者、审计人员、分析人员以及其他财务报表使用者们在会计原则与其具体应用之间架起一座桥梁。

金以文
会计专业咨询服务首席合伙人
普华永道中国及香港

How to use this publication

Given the increasing importance of IFRS in China and the continued convergence of CAS and IFRS, the Accounting Consulting Services team of PwC China and Hong Kong have undertaken a significant project to translate the IFRS Manual of Accounting into Chinese.

The Manual is a practical guide in applying IFRS and the views are based on the extensive experience of the PwC's global network of firms. However, IFRS is not static and is continuously developing. The views on its interpretation and application will adapt and evolve. The views expressed in this Manual are a guide to applying IFRS rather than a set of definitive interpretations. The application of IFRS requires significant judgement and specific facts and circumstances should be carefully considered.

IFRS Manual of Accounting with Chinese Translation will be released in different volumes. Depending on the topic, each release may be a chapter or a combination of a number of chapters from the Manual.

Because of the interdependencies between individual IFRS, there are many cross references between different chapters of the Manual. Although the IFRS Manual of Accounting with Chinese Translation will be released in different volumes, the cross references have been maintained. Users are encouraged to refer to those cross references in other translated chapters or to the English version of the Manual if it helps in their understanding.

This book is the thirteenth volume of IFRS Manual of Accounting Series with Chinese Translation. The content covers Chapter 33 – Service concession arrangements of the English version and its translation. While every effort has been made to ensure an accurate translation, reference should be made to the English version in the event there are any differences between the Chinese and English versions.

使用说明

鉴于 IFRS 在中国愈发重要以及 CAS 和 IFRS 的持续趋同，普华永道中国及香港的会计专业咨询服务小组已着手开始了一项具有重大意义的项目，即将《国际财务报告准则实务指引》译成中文。

《国际财务报告准则实务指引》是对应用 IFRS 的实务指引，其中的观点是基于普华永道全球成员机构网络丰富的经验。然而，IFRS 不是静止的，而是持续发展的；因此，对 IFRS 的解释和适用会有所改变和发展。本指引表达的观点是对应用 IFRS 的一种指引，而非一套具有决定性的解释。IFRS 的应用需要大量的判断，还应当谨慎考虑特定的事实及所处的环境。

IFRS 实务指引及其中文翻译版将分成多册发行。根据主题，每一册可能是本指引的某一章节或是包含某几个章节。

由于各个 IFRS 准则之间的相互依存，因此本指引中不同的章节会相互参照索引。尽管 IFRS 实务指引及其中文翻译版将分成多册发行，但仍保留此类相互参照索引。如果有助于理解，我们鼓励读者阅读此类相互参照索引时参考其他已翻译的章节或指引的英文版。

本书为普华永道国际财务报告准则实务指引系列（中英文对照）的第十三册。内容为英文原版的《国际财务报告准则实务指引》中的《第三十三章——特许服务权安排》。我们已尽最大的努力来确保翻译的准确，但中文翻译版与英文版出现不一致时，应参考英文版。

The chapters of our IFRS Manual of Accounting have been restructured in 2013 and changes have been marked as follow:

IFRS Manual of Accounting (MoA)

Accounting rules and principles

01 – Introduction

02 – Accounting principles and applicability of IFRS (combined with chapter 1 in MoA 2013)

03 – First-time adoption of IFRS

04 – Presentation of financial statements

05 – Accounting policies, accounting estimates and errors (chapter 3 in MoA 2013)

06 – Hyper-inflation (chapter 31 in MoA 2013)

07 – Foreign currencies

08 – Insurance contracts

Income statement and related notes

09 – Revenue and construction contracts

10 – Segment reporting

11 – Employee benefits

11A – Employee benefits (IAS 19 revised)

12 – Share-based payment

13 – Taxation

14 – Earnings per share

Balance sheet and related notes

15 – Intangible assets

16 – Property, plant and equipment

17 – Investment property

18 – Impairment of assets

19 – Lease accounting

20 – Inventories

英文原版《国际财务报告准则实务指引》的章节已在2013年再版时重新排列，变动已列示如下：

国际财务报告准则实务指引

会计规则和原则

01 – 引言

02 – 会计原则和国际财务报告准则的适用性（在2013版中与第一章合并）

03 – 首次采用国际财务报告准则

04 – 财务报表的列报

05 – 会计政策、会计估计和差错（在2013版中为第三章）

06 – 恶性通货膨胀（在2013版中为第三十一章）

07 – 外币

08 – 保险合同

利润表及相关附注

09 – 收入与建造合同

10 – 分部报告

11 – 职工福利

11A – 职工福利（IAS 19 修订版）

12 – 以股份为基础的支付（“股份支付”）

13 – 所得税会计

14 – 每股收益

资产负债表及相关附注

15 – 无形资产

16 – 不动产、工厂和设备

17 – 投资性房地产

18 – 资产减值

19 – 租赁会计

20 – 存货

Consolidated financial statements

Other subjects

IFRS Manual of Accounting—Financial Instruments (chapter 6 in MoA 2013)

合并财务报表

其他主题

国际财务报告准则实务指引——金融工具（在 2013 版中为第六章）

06 – Classification of financial instruments (chapter 6. 4 in MoA 2013)
07 – Financial liabilities and equity (chapter 6. 5 in MoA 2013)
08 – Recognition and derecognition (chapter 6. 6 in MoA 2013)
09 – Measurement of financial assets and liabilities (chapter 6. 7 in MoA 2013)
10 – Hedge accounting (chapter 6. 8 in MoA 2013)
11 – Presentation and disclosure (chapter 6. 9 in MoA 2013)
12 – IFRS 9, "Financial Instruments" (chapter 6. 10 in MoA 2013)

06 – 金融工具的分类（在 2013 版中为第 6. 4 章）

07 – 金融负债和权益（在 2013 版中为第 6. 5 章）

08 – 确认和终止确认（在 2013 版中为第 6. 6 章）

09 – 金融资产和金融负债的计量（在 2013 版中为第 6. 7 章）

10 – 套期会计（在 2013 版中为第 6. 8 章）

11 – 列报和披露（在 2013 版中为第 6. 9 章）

12 – 国际财务报告准则第 9 号——金融工具（在 2013 版中为第 6. 10 章）

International standards and interpretations

International standards

IFRS 1	First-time adoption of International Financial Reporting Standards
IFRS 2	Share-based payment
IFRS 3	Business combinations
IFRS 4	Insurance contracts
IFRS 5	Non-current assets held for sale and discontinued operations
IFRS 6	Exploration for and evaluation of mineral resources
IFRS 7	Financial instruments: Disclosures
IFRS 8	Operating segments
IFRS 9	Financial instruments
IFRS 10	Consolidated financial statements
IFRS 11	Joint arrangements
IFRS 12	Disclosure of interests in other entities
IFRS 13	Fair value measurement
IAS 1	Presentation of financial statements
IAS 2	Inventories
IAS 7	Cash flow statements
IAS 8	Accounting policies, changes in accounting estimates and errors
IAS 10	Events after the balance sheet date
IAS 11	Construction contracts
IAS 12	Income taxes
IAS 16	Property, plant and equipment
IAS 17	Leases
IAS 18	Revenue
IAS 19	Employee benefits
IAS 20	Accounting for government grants and disclosure of government assistance
IAS 21	The effects of changes in foreign exchange rates
IAS 23	Borrowing costs

国际财务报告准则及解释公告

国际财务报告准则

国际财务报告准则第 1 号	首次采用国际财务报告准则
国际财务报告准则第 2 号	以股份为基础的支付
国际财务报告准则第 3 号	企业合并
国际财务报告准则第 4 号	保险合同
国际财务报告准则第 5 号	持有待售的非流动资产和终止经营
国际财务报告准则第 6 号	矿产资源的勘探和评价
国际财务报告准则第 7 号	金融工具：披露
国际财务报告准则第 8 号	经营分部
国际财务报告准则第 9 号	金融工具
国际财务报告准则第 10 号	合并财务报表
国际财务报告准则第 11 号	合营安排
国际财务报告准则第 12 号	对其他主体中权益的披露
国际财务报告准则第 13 号	公允价值计量
国际会计准则第 1 号	财务报表的列报
国际会计准则第 2 号	存货
国际会计准则第 7 号	现金流量表
国际会计准则第 8 号	会计政策、会计估计变更和差错
国际会计准则第 10 号	报告期后事项
国际会计准则第 11 号	建造合同
国际会计准则第 12 号	所得税
国际会计准则第 16 号	不动产、工厂和设备
国际会计准则第 17 号	租赁
国际会计准则第 18 号	收入
国际会计准则第 19 号	职工福利
国际会计准则第 20 号	政府补助的会计和政府援助的披露
国际会计准则第 21 号	汇率变动的影响
国际会计准则第 23 号	借款费用

IAS 24	Related-party disclosures
IAS 26	Accounting and reporting by retirement benefit plans
IAS 27	Consolidated and separate financial statements
IAS 28	Investments in associates
IAS 29	Financial reporting in hyper-inflationary economies
IAS 31	Interests in joint ventures
IAS 32	Financial instruments: Presentation
IAS 33	Earnings per share
IAS 34	Interim financial reporting
IAS 36	Impairment of assets
IAS 37	Provisions, contingent liabilities and contingent assets
IAS 38	Intangible assets
IAS 39	Financial instruments: Recognition and measurement
IAS 40	Investment property
IAS 41	Agriculture

Interpretations

IFRIC 1	Changes in existing decommissioning, restoration and similar liabilities
IFRIC 2	Members' shares in co-operative entities and similar Instruments
IFRIC 4	Determining whether an arrangement contains a lease
IFRIC 5	Rights to interests arising from decommissioning, restoration and environmental rehabilitation funds
IFRIC 6	Liabilities arising from participating in a specific market - Waste electrical and electronic equipment
IFRIC 7	Applying the restatement approach under IAS 29 Financial reporting in hyper-inflationary economies
IFRIC 8	Scope of IFRS 2
IFRIC 9	Re-assessment of embedded derivatives
IFRIC 10	Interim financial reporting and impairment
IFRIC 11	IFRS 2 - Group and treasury share transactions
IFRIC 12	Service concession arrangements

国际会计准则第 24 号	关联方披露
国际会计准则第 26 号	退休福利计划的会计和报告
国际会计准则第 27 号	合并财务报表和单独财务报表
国际会计准则第 28 号	联营中的投资
国际会计准则第 29 号	恶性通货膨胀经济中的财务报告
国际会计准则第 31 号	合营中的权益
国际会计准则第 32 号	金融工具：列报
国际会计准则第 33 号	每股收益
国际会计准则第 34 号	中期财务报告
国际会计准则第 36 号	资产减值
国际会计准则第 37 号	准备、或有负债和或有资产
国际会计准则第 38 号	无形资产
国际会计准则第 39 号	金融工具：确认和计量
国际会计准则第 40 号	投资性房地产
国际会计准则第 41 号	农业

解释公告

国际财务报告解释公告第 1 号	现有退役、复原和类似负债的变动
国际财务报告解释公告第 2 号	成员在合作主体中的股份和类似工具
国际财务报告解释公告第 4 号	确定一项协议是否包含租赁
国际财务报告解释公告第 5 号	退役、复原和环境恢复基金产生的权益
国际财务报告解释公告第 6 号	参与废弃电器和电子设备特定市场产生的负债
国际财务报告解释公告第 7 号	应用《国际会计准则第 29 号——恶性通货膨胀经济中的财务报告》中的重述法
国际财务报告解释公告第 8 号	《国际财务报告准则第 2 号》的范围
国际财务报告解释公告第 9 号	嵌入衍生工具的重估
国际财务报告解释公告第 10 号	中期财务报告和减值
国际财务报告解释公告第 11 号	《国际财务报告准则第 2 号》：集团和库藏股交易
国际财务报告解释公告第 12 号	特许服务权安排

IFRIC 13	Customer loyalty programmes
IFRIC 14	IAS 19 – The limit on a defined benefit asset, minimum funding requirements and their interaction
IFRIC 15	Agreements for the construction of real estate
IFRIC 16	Hedges of a net investment in a foreign operation
IFRIC 17	Distributions of non-cash assets to owners
IFRIC 18	Transfers of assets from customers
IFRIC 19	Extinguishing financial liabilities with equity instruments
IFRIC 20	Stripping costs in the production phase of a surface mine
SIC 7	Introduction of the euro
SIC 10	Government Assistance – No specific relation to operating activities
SIC 12	Consolidation – Special purpose entities
SIC 13	Jointly controlled entities – Non-Monetary contributions by venturers
SIC 15	Operating leases – Incentives
SIC 21	Income taxes – Recovery of revalued non-depreciable assets
SIC 25	Income taxes – Changes in the tax status of an entity or its shareholders
SIC 27	Evaluating the substance of transactions in the legal form of a lease
SIC 29	Service Concession Arrangements: Disclosures
SIC 31	Revenue – Barter transactions involving advertising services
SIC 32	Intangible assets – Web site costs

国际财务报告解释公告第 13 号	客户忠诚度计划
国际财务报告解释公告第 14 号	《国际会计准则第 19 号》：对设定受益资产的限制、最低资金要求及其相互作用
国际财务报告解释公告第 15 号	房地产建造合同
国际财务报告解释公告第 16 号	对境外经营净投资的套期
国际财务报告解释公告第 17 号	以非现金资产对所有者进行分配
国际财务报告解释公告第 18 号	从客户处转移资产
国际财务报告解释公告第 19 号	以权益工具解除金融负债
国际财务报告解释公告第 20 号	露天矿生产阶段的剥离成本
国际会计准则解释公告第 7 号	引入欧元
国际会计准则解释公告第 10 号	政府援助：与经营活动没有特定联系的政府援助
国际会计准则解释公告第 12 号	合并：特殊目的主体
国际会计准则解释公告第 13 号	共同控制主体：合营者的非货币性投入
国际会计准则解释公告第 15 号	经营租赁：激励措施
国际会计准则解释公告第 21 号	所得税：已重估非折旧资产的收回
国际会计准则解释公告第 25 号	所得税：主体或其股东纳税状况的改变
国际会计准则解释公告第 27 号	评价涉及租赁法律形式的交易实质
国际会计准则解释公告第 29 号	特许服务权安排：披露
国际会计准则解释公告第 31 号	收入：涉及广告服务的易货交易
国际会计准则解释公告第 32 号	无形资产：网站成本

Abbreviations and terms used

Accounts	financial statements
AG	Application Guidance
App	Appendix
ARC	Accounting Regulatory Committee
BC	Basis for Conclusions (to an accounting standard)
C	currency unit
Chp	Chapter
chapter (1)	'PricewaterhouseCoopers' Manual of accounting' – chapter (1)
CESR	Committee of European Securities Regulators
CPP	current purchasing power
DP	discussion paper
EBIT	earnings before interest and tax
EBITDA	earnings before interest, tax, depreciation and amortisation
ED	exposure draft
EFRAG	European Financial Reporting Advisory Group
EPS	earnings per share
EU	European Union
FASB	Financial Accounting Standards Board (US)
Framework	Framework for the preparation and presentation of financial statements
GAAP	generally accepted accounting principles (and practices)
IAS	International Accounting Standard (see also IFRS)
IASB	International Accounting Standards Board
IFRIC	International Financial Reporting Interpretations Committee
IFRS	International Financial Reporting Standard (see also IAS)
IG	Implementation Guidance (to an accounting standard)

缩写及词汇对照

财务报表
实施指南
附录
会计监管委员会
(某一准则的) 结论基础
货币单位
章
第一章 (普华永道《国际财务报告准则实务指引》——第一章)

欧洲证券监管委员会
现行购买力
讨论稿
息税前收益
扣除利息、所得税、折旧和摊销之前的收益
征求意见稿
欧洲财务报告咨询组
每股收益
欧盟
(美国) 财务会计准则委员会
编报财务报表的框架

公认会计原则
国际会计准则 (亦请参见 IFRS)
国际会计准则理事会
国际财务报告解释委员会
国际财务报告准则 (亦请参见 IAS)
(某一准则的) 应用指南

para(s)	paragraph(s) of Schedules to the Companies Acts, or IFRSs or IASs or FRSs, or SSAPs, or FREDs, or EDs, or DPs, or text
PPE	property, plant and equipment
US SEC	US Securities and Exchange Commission
SIC	Standing Interpretation Committee of the IASC (see IFRIC)
SPE	special purpose entity
UK	United Kingdom
US	United States of America

段落（公司法、国际财务报告准则、国际会计准则、财务报告准则、会计实务准则、财务报告征求意见稿、征求意见稿、讨论稿或文章中的段落）

不动产、工厂和设备
美国证券交易委员会
国际会计准则委员会的常设解释委员会（参见 IFRIC）

特殊目的主体
英国
美国

Chapter 33 Service concession arrangements

Contents

第三十三章　特许服务权安排

目　录

Introduction

33. 1 National governments are generally responsible for the construction, operation and maintenance of infrastructure for public services such as roads, railways, bridges, schools, hospitals, prisons, airports, water distribution and waste management systems, energy supply and telecommunication networks. Such public services are traditionally financed by the public. However, in recent years, some countries have developed private finance initiative (PFI) and public private partnership (PPP) arrangements under which the public sector is able to procure the provision of such public services from the private sector. These arrangements, referred to generally as 'service concession arrangements', have in some countries become an important part of the government's strategy for improving public infrastructure and delivering high quality public services.

33. 2 It is integral to most service concession arrangements that the private sector designs, builds, finances and operates the infrastructure in order to provide the contracted services. The private sector operators are required to bid for the contract, thus allowing competition to enter into the market. By requiring the private sector to put its own capital at risk and to deliver clear levels of service to the public over the long-term, the government aims to deliver high quality public services and ensure that public assets are delivered on time and to budget, without having to raise taxes to fund the infrastructure.

33. 3 There is currently no specific IFRS that applies to service concession arrangements. IFRIC 12 interprets various standards in setting out the accounting requirements for service concession arrangements, while SIC 29 contains disclosure requirement.

Features of a service concession arrangements

33. 4 A service concession arrangement generally involves a government or other public sector entity (referred to as the grantor) conveying to a private

引言

33.1 国家政府通常负责公路、铁路、桥梁、学校、医院、监狱、机场、用水配送和垃圾管理系统、能源供应和电信网络等公共服务基础设施的建造、经营和维护。传统上，这些公共服务是由公众融资。不过，近年来一些国家出现了私营主动融资（private finance initiative）和公私合作关系（public private partnership）安排，在这些安排下，公共部门能够从私营部门采购此类公共服务。这些安排通常称为“特许服务权安排”，在一些国家已成为政府改善公共设施、提供高品质公共服务战略的重要组成部分。

33.2 为提供合同所规定的服务，在大多数特许服务权安排中，私营部门整合设计、建设、融资并经营基础设施项目是必须的。私营部门经营方必须竞标合同，从而为市场引入竞争机制。通过要求私营部门承担自身资本风险，并向公众长期提供层次分明的服务，政府的目标是提供高品质的公共服务，并确保公共资产准时按预算到位，而不需要提高税收来为基础设施项目融资。

33.3 目前没有特定的国际财务报告准则适用于特许服务权安排。IFRIC 12 阐释了各个准则对特许服务权安排的会计处理要求，而 SIC 29 则包含了有关披露要求。

特许服务权安排的特征

33.4 特许服务权安排通常涉及一个政府部门或其他公共部门实体（称为授予方）向私营部门实体（称为经营方）让渡某一时间段的下列特许权：

sector entity (referred to as the operator) for the period of the concession the following:

- The right to provide services that give the public access to major economic and social facilities. Such facilities typically involve the use of infrastructure such as those mentioned in paragraph 33.1 above. The services provided by the operator often include the construction of the infrastructure or its upgrade (for example, by increasing its capacity) and the operation and maintenance of that infrastructure for the period of the concession. These arrangements are referred to in IFRIC 12 as 'build-operate-transfer' (BOT) and 'rehabilitate-operate-transfer' (ROT) arrangements.

- The operator is remunerated for its services, either directly by the grantor or given the right to charge users during the period of the arrangement. In some instances, the operator may be remunerated by both the grantor and the public. In almost all instances, income is received by the operator once the infrastructure is brought into use under a BOT or ROT arrangement.

- The arrangement is governed by contract or regulation, which typically sets out the terms and conditions for providing the service, including standards of performance, payment mechanism and adjustments to payments during the concession period and arrangements for settling disputes.

- The operator is obliged to hand over the infrastructure to the grantor in a specified condition at the end of the period of the arrangement, irrespective of which party initially financed it.

Objectives and scope of IFRIC 12

Objectives

33.5 IFRIC 12's objective is to establish general principles on recognising and measuring the obligations and related rights in service concession arrangements. Requirements for disclosing information about service concession arrangements are dealt with in SIC 29. The issues addressed in IFRIC 12 are:

■ 向公众提供服务以方便其使用主要经济和社会设施的权利。这些设施通常涉及诸如上述第 33.1 段提及的基础设施的使用。经营方提供的服务通常包括基础设施建造或者改进（如增加产能）以及特许权期间基础设施的经营和维护。这些安排在 IFRIC 12 中称为“建造 – 运营 – 转移”（BOT）和“复原 – 运营 – 转移”（ROT）。

■ 经营方提供服务的报酬或直接来自授予方，或获得授权在特许权安排期间向使用者收费。在有些情况下，经营方既可能从授予方获得报酬，又可能从公众获得报酬。几乎所有情况下，BOT 和 ROT 安排下的基础设施一旦投入使用，经营方就有了收益。

■ 安排受合同或监管的约束，通常设定提供服务的条款和条件，包括业绩标准、支付机制、在特许权期间付款的调整以及解决争端的安排。

■ 经营方有义务在安排期间结束时，按规定条件向授予方移交基础设施，而无论最初系由何方出资。

IFRIC 12 的目标和范围

目标

33.5　IFRIC 12 的目标是为特许服务权安排的义务和相关权利的确认和计量确立普遍原则。有关特许服务权安排信息披露要求参见 SIC 29。IFRIC 12 中探讨的相关问题如下：

- The treatment of the operator's right over the infrastructure.
- Recognition and measurement of consideration.
- Construction or upgrade services.
- Operation services.
- Borrowing costs.
- Subsequent accounting treatment of a financial asset and an intangible asset.
- Items provided to the operator by the grantor.

[IFRIC 12 para 10].

Scope

33.6 Private participation in the provision of public services can take many forms. The nature and provisions of the contract vary by industry sector. The legal frameworks under which such arrangements are carried out also vary from country to country. The IFRIC noted that a considerable amount of time and effort would be needed to provide comprehensive guidance that would cover all such situations. So the IFRIC agreed that the interpretation should deal only with accounting by the operator for construction of new infrastructure, the acquisition of infrastructure from a third party and for use of existing infrastructure of the grantor; and that it should be restricted to service concession arrangements in which there is an obligation to provide services to the public.

33.7 The scope of IFRIC 12 is limited to the accounting by operators for public-to-private service concession arrangements that are controlled by the grantor. The grantor is able to control the use of the infrastructure and, hence, the service concession arrangement will fall within IFRIC 12's scope if both the conditions set out below are met. This would apply even if the operator holds legal title to the infrastructure.

- the grantor controls or regulates what services the operator must provide with the infrastructure, to whom it must provide them, and at what price; and
- the grantor controls – through ownership, beneficial entitlement or otherwise – any significant residual interest in the infrastructure at the end of the

■ 经营方对基础设施的权利的处理。

■ 对价的确认和计量。

■ 建造或改良服务。

■ 运营服务。

■ 借款费用。

■ 金融资产和无形资产的后续会计处理。

■ 授予方向经营方提供的项目。

［IFRIC 12 第 10 段］。

范围

33.6　私营实体参与提供公共服务可采取多种形式。合同的性质和规定因行业部门不同而有所不同。此类安排所采用的法律框架各国也有所不同。国际财务报告解释委员会指出，提供能涵盖所有情况的综合性指导原则需要投入大量的时间和精力。所以，国际财务报告解释委员会同意其解释应当只涉及经营方的新建基础设施、从第三方收购基础设施以及利用授予方现有基础设施的会计处理，而且其解释也应该仅限于有义务向公众提供服务的特许服务权安排。

33.7　IFRIC 12 仅限于由授予方控制的公共 – 私营特许服务权安排之经营方的会计处理。授予方能控制基础设施的使用，因而，如果同时满足下列两个条件，该特许服务权安排属于 IFRIC 12 的范围。即使经营方对基础设施拥有合法所有权，此解释同样适用。

■ 授予方控制或管制经营方利用基础设施必须提供的服务类型、提供服务的对象和服务的价格；以及

■ 在服务安排期末，授予方通过所有权、收益权或其他形式控制所有基础设施的重大剩余权益。

arrangement's term.

[IFRIC 12 para 5(a)(b)].

The issue of control is discussed further from paragraph 33.15 below.

33.8 IFRIC 12 does not specify the accounting by grantors. [IFRIC 12 para 9]. This is because the IFRIC's objective and priority was to establish guidance for operators. Furthermore, in many cases the grantor is a government body and IFRSs are not designed to apply to such entities, though such entities may find them appropriate.

Public service obligation

33.9 As noted above, IFRIC 12's scope is limited to public-to-private service concession arrangements. A key feature of these service concession arrangements is the public service nature of the obligation undertaken by the operator. Public policy is for services related to the infrastructure to be provided to the public, irrespective of the identity of the party that operates the service. [IFRIC 12 para 3].

33.10 It is not clear what is meant by 'the public service nature of the obligation'. In normal parlance, 'public service' is generally taken to mean services that are provided by government to its citizens. The purpose of providing such services is to meet the citizens' basic needs that are conducive to modern living and also to cater for their fundamental rights (for example, the right to clean water). In other words, such services are considered so essential to modern life that for moral reasons their provision is guaranteed. Hence, they are available to all. Public services generally include health care, education, gas, electricity, water, waste management, public transportation, public broadcasting, fire services, telecommunications and social housing. Such services have traditionally not been provided by the private sector (for example, following a privatisation) as they are the primary responsibility of national governments. Even where they are provided by the private sector, for social and political reasons they are usually subject to regulation going beyond that applying to most economic sectors.

［IFRIC 12 第 5（a）（b）段］。

控制权问题将在下面第 33.15 段起作进一步讨论。

33.8　IFRIC 12 并没有规定授予方的会计核算。［IFRIC 12 第 9 段］。这是因为国际财务报告解释委员会的目标和优先考虑的事项是要为经营方确立指导原则。再者，许多情况下授予方是政府机构，而国际财务报告准则并非为适用这样的主体而设计，尽管上述主体可能认为其适用相关准则。

公共服务的义务

33.9　如上所述，IFRIC 12 的适用范围仅限于公共－私营特许服务权安排。这些特许服务权安排的一项关键特征是具有公共服务性质的义务要由经营方来承担。公共政策是为公众提供基础设施相关的服务，与服务运营方的身份无关。［IFRIC 12 第 3 段］。

33.10　“公共服务性质的义务”内涵并未清晰定义。按常规说法，“公共服务”一般是指由政府提供给公民的服务。提供这类服务的目的是为了满足公民的基本需求，有益于建设现代化生活，同时也为了保障其基本权利（例如，获取清洁饮水的权利）。换言之，这类服务对于现代生活而言至关重要，从道德上讲必须保障供应。因而，这类服务是对全民开放的。公共服务一般包括医疗、教育、煤气、电力、自来水、垃圾处理、公共交通、公共广播、消防、电信以及保障性住房。这类服务传统上并不是由私营部门提供的（例如，实行私有化之后），因为这是国家政府的主要责任。即使这类服务有时是由私营部门提供，由于社会和政治原因，其所受到的监管通常要比大部分经济部门严格。

33.11 SIC 29 states that a service concession arrangement generally involves the grantor conveying to the operator for the period of the concession the right to provide services that give the public access to major economic and social facilities. It would, therefore, appear that any infrastructure (irrespective of its nature) that is made available for public use (whether for the provision of basic necessities such as water, electricity, gas, transport, hospitals, schools, etc; or for social reasons such as zoos, swimming pools, sports stadium, etc) under an arrangement between a public body and a private entity involves a public service obligation. In other words, as the services provided using the infrastructure are provided to the public, and public policy in that jurisdiction requires these services are provided to the public, they fall within IFRIC 12's scope. It is irrelevant whether the public chooses to use the infrastructure, or is required to do so, as long as the infrastructure is available for public use. Furthermore, the public service obligation may vary from country to country. What is deemed to be a public service in a developed country, or vice versa, may not be viewed as a public service in a developing country for social or political reasons.

33.12 IFRIC 12 acknowledges that it is not necessary for the operator to provide services directly to the public for the arrangement to fall within its scope. [IFRIC 12 para 3]. This means that the public service obligation undertaken by the private sector entity could be limited to constructing the infrastructure and maintaining it in a proper state. The actual service to the general public could be provided by another party, as long as that public service is provided using the infrastructure that has been constructed and maintained by the private sector operator. An example is where the operator builds and maintains a hospital building, but the government uses the hospital building to provide medical services directly to the general public.

33.13 Conversely, when the infrastructure is not available for the public to use, a public service obligation does not exist and the arrangement is not within the interpretation's scope. An example is an information technology outsourcing contract that is awarded to a private entity by a government department. Other situations referred to in SIC 29 that are not service concession arrangements include an entity outsourcing the operation of its internal services (for example, employee cafeteria, building maintenance

33.11 SIC 29 指出，特许服务权安排一般涉及授予方在特许期间内向经营方让渡提供服务的权利，以便公众能使用主要的经济和社会设施。因而，公共机构与私营实体间特许权安排之下的任何可供公众使用（无论是满足基本需求，如自来水、电力、煤气、交通、医院、学校等，还是出于社会因素的考虑，诸如动物园、游泳池、体育馆等）的基础设施（无论其性质），似乎都涉及公共服务的义务问题。换言之，由于使用基础设施来提供的服务是要提供给公众的，该管辖权内的公共政策要求这些服务向公众开放，因而其属于 IFRIC 12 适用的范围。只要基础设施向公众开放，而与公众是否选择使用或被要求使用上述基础设施无关。此外，公共服务的义务可能因国家而异。在发达国家被认为是公共服务的项目，在发展中国家，出于社会和政治原因，或许不被认为是公共服务，反之亦然。

33.12 IFRIC 12 指出，不必一定要由经营方直接向公众提供服务，才会使这个安排落入 IFRIC 12 的范围中。[IFRIC 12 第 3 段]。这意味着私营部门实体所承担的公共服务义务可仅限于基础设施建设，并使其保持良好状态。只要提供公共服务所用的基础设施是由私营部门经营方建设和维护，可由另一方向公众提供实际服务。例如，经营方建设和维护一幢医院大楼，但由政府利用该医院大楼直接向公众提供医疗服务。

33.13 相反，如果基础设施不向公众开放，那么公共服务的义务也就不存在，因而该安排就不属于此解释的范围。例如由政府部门授予私营实体的信息技术外包合同。SIC 29 提到的不属于特许服务权安排的情况包括实体外包其内部服务运营（例如，员工餐厅、建筑维修以及会计职能）。

and accounting functions).

Decision tree for arrangements falling within IFRIC 12's scope

33. 14 IFRIC 12 provides a decision tree for determining whether a public-to-private service concession arrangement would fall within its scope. This is reproduced below:

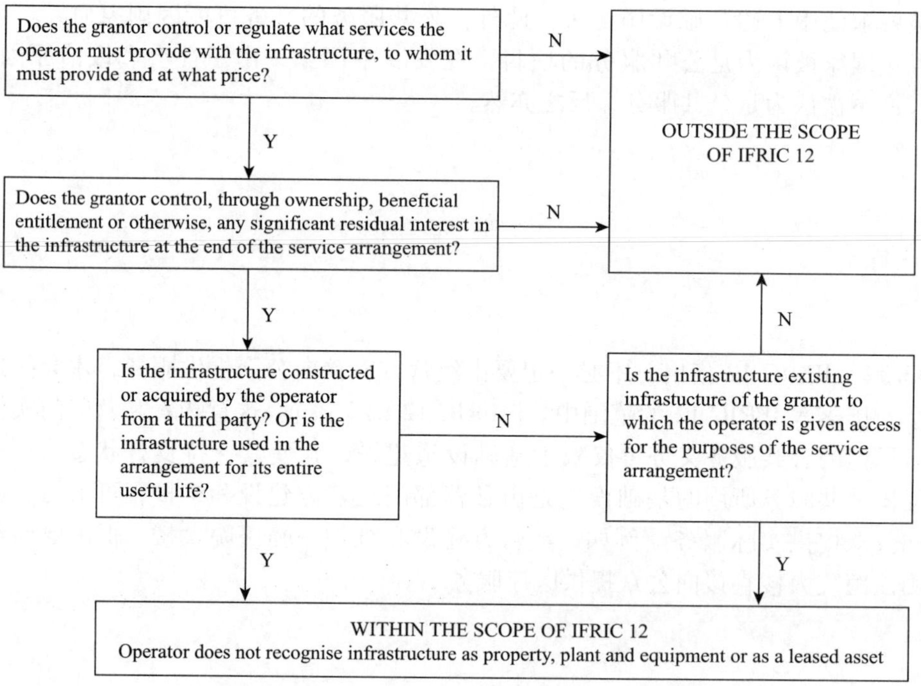

[IFRIC 12 – Information note 1].

Control or regulation of services

33. 15 The control or regulation of services referred to in the first condition of paragraph 33. 7 above does not have to be by contract (an agreement or a licence). The grantor may control the services through some other form of regulation. Control also includes circumstances where the grantor buys all of the output as well as those in which it is bought by other users. In applying this condition, the

属于 IFRIC 12 范围的安排决策树

33.14　IFRIC 12 提供了决策树，以确定某个公共－私营特许服务权安排是否属于其范围。图表再现如下：

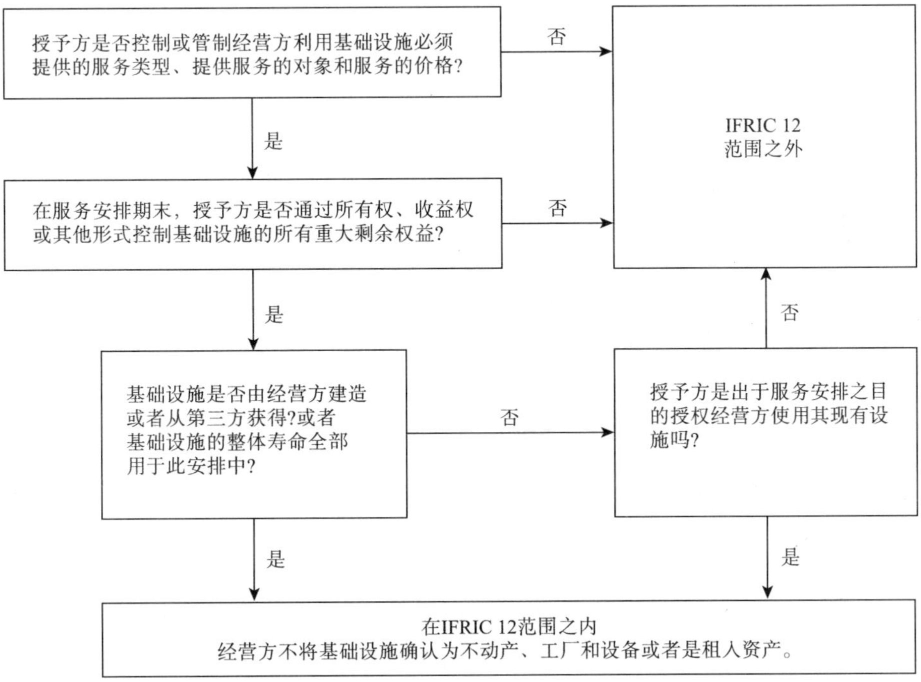

［IFRIC 12——信息附注 1］。

服务控制或监管

33.15　上面第 33.7 段中的第一个条件提及的服务控制或监管并不一定是通过合同（协议或使用许可）。授予方可能通过某些其他监管手段控制服务。此外，控制手段包括授予方购买所有的产品，以及其他用户购买全部产品的情况。为了应用这一条件，授予方及任何相关方的因素必须一并考虑。如果授予方是公共部门实体，那么公共部门整体，与任何代表公众利益的监管者一

grantor and any related parties must be considered together. If the grantor is a public sector entity, the public sector as a whole, together with any regulators acting in the public interest, are to be regarded as related to the grantor. [IFRIC 12 para AG2]. This is fairly common in the utility sector (for example, supply of water or electricity). Another example would be an entity that provides a national railway network as a monopoly supplier of public service that is monitored by an independent regulator as to pricing and compliance with the terms of the licence granted by the government. In such circumstances, the government and the independent regulator together are considered as the grantor.

Control of pricing

33. 16 For the purposes of the first condition in paragraph 33. 7 above, the term 'price' refers to the amount that the grantor pays to the operator for providing the public service or the amount that the operator charges the general public for the services provided. Obviously, where the grantor has complete control over the price charged by the operator, the first condition of control in paragraph 33. 7 above is met. However, it is not necessary for the grantor to have complete control of the price. It is sufficient for the price to be regulated by the grantor, contract or the regulator. [IFRIC 12 para AG3].

33. 17 There are various ways in which prices are set or regulated by the grantor or a regulator. These may range from fixed price arrangements to those that are based on a formula up to a maximum price and no more. The formula may be linked to performance that is within the operator's control or linked to an index, such as the RPI or CPI, which is neither within the control of the grantor nor the operator. As long as the basis or the framework under which the prices are set are subject to regulation, the pricing element of the first control test in paragraph 33. 7 above is met.

33. 18 In some circumstances, the grantor may control or regulate the price through a capping mechanism. In such circumstances, it would be necessary to look at the arrangement's substance. Consequently, a cap that will apply only in remote circumstances has no substance and will be ignored. Similarly, other features of a pricing mechanism that are deemed to be non-substantive in nature

起，被认为是授予方的关联方。[IFRIC 12 AG 第 2 段]。这在公用事业部门非常常见（如供水或供电）。另一个例子是提供全国性铁路网的实体，作为公共服务垄断供应商，其定价以及是否遵守政府颁发的授权许可条款受到独立监管者的监督。在此情况下，政府与独立监管者一起，被认为是授予方。

定价控制

33.16　就上述第 33.7 段中的第一个条件的目的而言，“价格”一词是指授予方为经营方提供公共服务所支付的金额，或是经营方为其提供的服务向公众收取的金额。很明显，如果授予方完全控制经营方的收费价格，那么上述第 33.7 段中的第一个控制条件便得以满足。然而，授予方无需完全控制价格。价格通过授予方、合同或监管者被控制即已足够。[IFRIC 12 AG 第 3 段]。

33.17　授予方或监管者设定和监管价格的手段多种多样。其范围可能从固定价格安排，到基于公式计算的各项限价安排。公式可与经营方控制范围内的业绩挂钩，或者与某一指数挂钩，如零售物价指数或者消费者物价指数，上述指数既不在授予方也不在经营方的控制范围内。只要定价基础或框架是受到监管约束的，价格因素即符合上述第 33.7 段中的第一个控制测试的要求。

33.18　在某些情况下，授予方也可能通过限价机制来控制和监管价格。在这种情况下，有必要看一下安排的实质。因此，只有在极少见的情况下才会适用的限价无实质意义，可以忽略不计。类似地，在本质上被认为无实质意义的定价机制的其他功能也应该忽略不计。有时合同可能给予经营方定价的自由，但任何超出最低商定金额的超额利润要返还给授予方。此种情况下，经

should also be ignored. Sometimes a contract may give the operator freedom to set its prices, but any excess profit over an agreed minimum is clawed back by the grantor. In such a case the operator's return is capped and the first control condition in paragraph 33.7 above is met. [IFRIC 12 para AG3].

Example – Control of pricing

The government of U owns the electricity generating and distribution company. It enters into a contract with a private sector operator under which the operator is required to maintain and operate the entire distribution network (including the national grid) for a period of 20 years. The operator earns revenue from charging customers directly for electricity supplied. The price per kilowatt-hour (kWh) of electricity charged is made up as shown below.

- Component 1 comprises a fixed price per kWh and is regulated by the government or its designated regulator.
- Component 2 comprises a distribution charge per kWh for transporting the electricity from the power station to the national network/grid. This component is subject to a capping mechanism by the regulator.
- Component 3 comprises a price per kWh that includes the operator's margin/return and is unregulated.

In the above example, since part of the totalprice per unit is unregulated (component 3) and the operator has the freedom to set this component of the total price per unit, the final price per unit charged by the operator is effectively unregulated. It follows that such a pricing mechanism would not meet the first condition in paragraph 33.7 above.

On the other hand, if component 3 of the pricing structure is regulated by the government through a capping mechanism, the final price per unit falls to be wholly regulated and the price element of the control test is met.

Control of residual interest

33.19 The second condition of control in paragraph 33.7 above is satisfied if

营方的收益被限定，符合上述第 33. 7 段中的第一个控制条件。[IFRIC 12 AG 第 3 段]。

示例——定价控制

U 政府拥有发电和配电公司。与私营部门经营方订立的合同要求经营方在 20 年的时间里，维护和运营整个输电网络（包括全国电网）。经营方供电所得的收入来自于直接向客户收费。每度（千瓦时）电收费价格构成如下：

- 组成部分 1 包含每度电固定价格，并受政府或其指定监管者的监管。
- 组成部分 2 包含将电力从发电站输送到全国性网络/电网的每度电配送费用。这部分价格受限于监管者确定的限价机制。
- 组成部分 3 包括含有经营方毛利/回报的每度电价格，而此价格是不受监管的。

在上述示例中，由于总单价的某些部分是不受监管的（组成部分 3），而经营方有设定此总单价组成部分的自由，因而经营方收取的最终单价实际上是不受监管的。因此，这样的定价机制并不符合上述第 33. 7 段中的第一个条件。

另一方面，如果组成部分 3 的定价结构由政府通过限价机制进行监管，那么最终单价完全受到监管，符合控制测试的价格因素。

剩余权益的控制

33. 19　如果授予方*控制基础设施的任何重大剩余权益*，则符合上述第 33. 7

the grantor *controls any significant residual interest* in the infrastructure asset. Again, if the grantor is a public sector entity, the public sector as a whole is regarded as related to the grantor. [IFRIC 12 para AG2]. The significant residual interest criterion is met where the grantor has a continuing right of use of the infrastructure throughout the concession period and restricts the operator's ability to sell or pledge the infrastructure. The residual interest in the infrastructure is the infrastructure's estimated current value as if it were already of the age and in the condition expected at the end of the period of the arrangement. [IFRIC 12 para AG4].

33.20 There are a number of ways in which a grantor can control the residual interest in the infrastructure. The most obvious is direct ownership where the grantor owns the infrastructure from the outset, but simply gives the operator a right of access to the infrastructure to undertake the public service during the concession period. Another arrangement is where the operator uses its own finance to build the infrastructure, but the grantor is able to control the residual interest through the concession agreement by requiring the operator to return the infrastructure at the end of the concession period or to hand it over to another operator. This type of arrangement is fairly common with many service concession arrangements using long-lived infrastructure assets.

33.21 Another way in which the grantor is able to exercise control of the residual infrastructure is through a call option to acquire the infrastructure asset at the end of the concession period. Such a call option would effectively prevent the operator from selling or pledging the asset. This means that the grantor has full control of the right to use the infrastructure throughout the concession period and, hence, the second condition of the control test is met. It does not matter whether the option exercise price is at fair value at the date of exercise (where the operator bears the residual value risk) or is pre-determined (where the grantor bears the residual value risk). The fact that the call option allows the grantor to control the right to use the infrastructure and, hence, its residual is sufficient for the concession arrangement to fall within IFRIC 12's scope. The control concept that is predominant in IFRIC 12 is wholly-distinct from the risks and rewards of ownership concept that forms the basis of accounting for public-to-private service arrangements in some national GAAPs. This issue is considered further from

段中的第二个控制条件。再次说明，如果授予方是公共部门实体，那么公共部门整体应视为与授予方相关联。[IFRIC 12 AG 第 2 段]。如果授予方在整个特许权期间对基础设施有持续使用权，并对经营方出售或抵押基础设施的能力进行限制，则符合重大剩余权益标准。基础设施的剩余权益是假定其已处在安排期末时的寿命和预期状况时所估计的现行价值 [IFRIC 12 AG 第 4 段]。

33.20　授予方可通过多种方式控制基础设施剩余权益。最为显而易见的是直接的所有权，即授予方从一开始就拥有基础设施，只是授予经营方使用基础设施的权利，以便其在特许权协议期间从事公共服务。另一类安排是经营方自行筹资建设基础设施，但授予方在特许权安排中要求经营方在特许权安排期末交还基础设施或将其移交另一经营方，从而控制剩余权益。这一类型的安排对于使用长期基础设施资产的特许服务权安排是相当常见的。

33.21　授予方能够通过另外一种方式实施剩余权益的控制权，即通过购入期权在特许权协议期末收购基础设施资产。该购入期权能够有效阻止经营方出售或抵押资产。这意味着授予方在整个特许权协议期间对基础设施的使用拥有完全控制权，因而符合控制测试的第二个条件。行权价格是行权当日的公允价值（由经营方承担剩余价值风险），还是预先设定（由授予方承担剩余价值风险）都无关紧要。购入期权使授予方能够控制基础设施的使用权，因此，其剩余权益足以使该特许权安排落入 IFRIC 12 的范围。IFRIC 12 中主要的控制概念，与所有权概念风险和回报相去甚远，而后一概念形成了一些国家一般公认会计原则中公共 - 私营特许服务权安排的会计基础。这个问题从下述第 33.39 段起做进一步讨论。

paragraph 33. 39 below.

33. 22 It should be noted that the second condition of control refers to ' significant residual interest' at the end of the arrangement's term. Determining what is a significant residual interest will often depend on the nature of the infrastructure asset. For example, a residual interest is likely to be significant where the infrastructure asset, such as a hospital building or prison, handed back at the end of the concession period still has a fairly long useful life. For other cash generating infrastructure assets such as toll roads or bridges, an estimate of the future cash flows would normally be used to assess the significance of the residual interest. Therefore, where a significant residual interest exists and that interest is required to be passed on to the grantor, the residual interest criterion is obviously met. Indeed, it is not uncommon for service concession arrangements to require the grantor to make a payment to the operator at the end of the concession period where the infrastructure asset has a fairly long useful life. Such payments may be at fair value where the operator bears a significant residual value risk. However, this does not preclude the arrangement from being within IFRIC 12's scope as long as the grantor has a continuing right of use of the infrastructure throughout the concession period and restricts the operator's ability to sell or pledge the infrastructure.

33. 23 Similarly, it is not necessary for the residual interest in the infrastructure handed over to the grantor at the end of the arrangement to be actually significant. For instance, ' whole-of-life ' assets (infrastructure used in a public-to-private service concession arrangement for its entire useful life) fall within IFRIC 12's scope, even though the residual interest at the end of their useful life is likely to be insignificant. This would apply even if the operator has legal title to the infrastructure at the end of the concession period. For a service arrangement to be within IFRIC 12's scope, it is necessary for the grantor to control any significant residual interest, as indicated above.

33. 24 It should be noted that the ' residual interest ' requirement of the control feature is generally present in service concessions, but not in many regulated industries, which properly recognise infrastructure assets as their own. Indeed, in many regulated industries, such as electricity, transport and water, there is no

33.22　应当指出，控制的第二个条件涉及该安排期末的“重大剩余权益”。决定何为重大剩余权益通常取决于基础设施资产的性质。例如，诸如医院建筑或监狱等基础设施资产，于特许权期间结束时交还仍有很长使用寿命，其剩余权益很可能是重大的。对于其他能产生现金的基础设施资产，诸如收费公路和桥梁而言，未来现金流量的估算通常用来评估剩余权益的重大性。因此，如果有剩余权益存在，而该权益又被要求交予授予方，那么其很明显符合剩余权益标准。实际上，对于特许服务权安排而言，在特许权期末基础设施资产尚有很长使用寿命的情况下，要求授予方向经营方支付费用也较常见。在经营方承担重大剩余价值风险的情况下，这笔付款可能以公允价值计量。然而，这并未将该安排排除在 IFRIC 12 范围之外，只要授予方在整个特许权期间对基础设施有持续使用权，并限制经营方出售或抵押该基础设施的能力即可。

33.23　类似地，在协议结束时交予授予方的基础设施剩余权益实际上不一定是重大的。例如，“整个使用寿命”资产（整个使用寿命期间都在公共－私营特许服务权安排中被使用的基础设施）就属于 IFRIC 12 的范围，即使在其使用寿命结束时剩余权益并不重大。即使特许权期间结束时经营方对于基础设施拥有合法的所有权，一样适用。服务安排如要属于 IFRIC 12 的范围，如上所述，授予方控制任何重大剩余权益是必要的。

33.24　应当指出，控制特征的“剩余权益”要求通常出现在特许服务权中，而在许多受监管的行业则没有，这些行业完全地将基础设施资产确认为自有资产。实际上，在许多受监管的行业，如电力、交通运输以及供水等，无义务在协议期末交还基础设施。这些基础设施只在例外的情况下才归还予授予

obligation to hand back the infrastructure at the end of the arrangement. Such infrastructure would revert to the grantor only in exceptional circumstances, for example, where there is a major breach of the conditions pertaining to the arrangement. But this does not necessarily indicate that the grantor controls the regulated utility.

33.25 In certain service arrangements, the operator may be required to replace part of an item of infrastructure asset that is used up in the service concession. For example, the operator may be required to resurface a toll road or the roof of a hospital building during the life of the agreement. In these types of arrangements, the residual interest criterion is met for the whole of the infrastructure (what the IFRIC refers to as a 'holistic' approach), including the part that is replaced, if the grantor controls any significant residual interest in the final replacement of that part. [IFRIC 12 para AG6].

33.26 A question arises as to whether a holistic approach, such as that described in the previous paragraph, would also apply in circumstances where the infrastructure includes physically separate items that were replaced during the life of the concession. If the items did not generate income separately from the infrastructure as a whole, we believe a holistic approach should be applied so that the residual interest criterion in paragraph 33.7 above is met if the infrastructure as a whole had a significant residual value, which was controlled by the grantor. The alternative of treating these items separately in accordance with IAS 16 could lead to any newly constructed items being treated as the operator's assets, if they were to be replaced over the life of the concession, unless there was a finance lease of those items from the operator to the grantor. However, over the life of a concession arrangement, replacement of significant items of newly constructed infrastructure are likely to be less frequent. More often, the replacement of significant infrastructure items would occur when the operator inherited an ageing infrastructure from the grantor, which it was obliged to replace under the arrangement's terms. In these circumstances, if the first condition in paragraph 33.7 above is met, the asset contributed by the grantor would not be an asset of the operator while the second condition would be met for the replacement infrastructure if it would revert to the grantor with a significant residual value, which was controlled by the grantor. Thus old and replacement infrastructure are treated

方，例如，严重违反与协议有关的条件。但这并不一定说明授予方控制着受监管的公用事业。

33.25　在某些服务协议中，可能要求经营方替换基础设施资产项目在特许服务权中耗尽的部分。例如，可能会要求经营方在协议期内为收费公路重铺路面，或者为医院大楼翻新屋顶。在这类协议中，如果授予方控制该最终更换部分的任何重大剩余权益，则整个基础设施（国际财务报告解释委员会所指的“整体”法），包括被更换的部分，均符合剩余权益标准。[IFRIC 12 AG 第6段]。

33.26　问题在于，如上段所述，整体法是否也适用于当基础设施包括特许权期间更换的实体上相分离的项目的情况。如果该项目并未独立于基础设施整体而产生收入，在基础设施作为一个整体具有重大剩余权益，且被授予方所控制的情况下，我们认为应该采用整体法，以符合上述第33.7段中的剩余权益标准。根据IAS 16的规定，如果项目在特许权期内被更换，除非经营方将这些项目融资租赁给授予方，对上述项目单独进行处理所选用的方法可能导致任何新建项目被处理为运营商的资产。然而，在特许服务权期内，新建基础设施重大项目的更换可能不那么频繁。更多的情况是，重大基础设施项目的更换会发生在经营方从授予方处继承陈旧的基础设施，而根据协议的条款其有义务进行更换的情况。在此情况下，如果符合上述第33.7段中的第一个条件，授予方所提供的资产将不会是经营方的资产，而如果将更换的基础设施归还于授予方，且该基础设施仍有重大剩余价值，且由授予方控制，则满足第二个条件。这样，对陈旧的和更换的基础设施的会计处理是一致的，从而避免了需要根据IAS 16的规定，对基础设施不同的组成部分进行会计处理。

consistently, thereby avoiding the need to account for different components of the infrastructure under IAS 16.

Infrastructure assets within scope

33.27 The interpretation applies to two groups of infrastructure assets that are used for the purposes of the service arrangements. These are:

- Infrastructure that the operator constructs or acquires from a third party for the purposes of the service arrangement. Where the infrastructure is subject to a tailored finance lease with a third partylessor, the infrastructure should be deemed acquired infrastructure.
- Existing infrastructure to which the grantor gives the operator access for the purpose of the service arrangement.

[IFRIC 12 para 7].

Partially regulated assets

33.28 In some service concession arrangements, the use of infrastructure is partly regulated by the grantor in the manner described in the first condition of paragraph 33.7 above and partly unregulated. Although these arrangements can take a variety of forms, IFRIC 12 considers two situations noted below:

- Any infrastructure that is physically separable and capable of being operated independently and meets the definition of a cash-generating unit in IAS 36 should be analysed separately if it is used wholly for unregulated purposes. For example, this might apply to a private wing of a hospital, where the remainder of the hospital is used by the grantor to treat public patients.
- When purely ancillary activities (such as a hospital shop) are unregulated, the control tests should be applied as if those services did not exist, because in cases in which the grantor controls the services in the manner described in paragraph 33.7 above, the existence of ancillary activities does not detract from the grantor's control of the infrastructure.

范围内的基础设施资产

33.27　此解释适用于用作特许服务权安排之目的的两组基础设施资产。它们是：

- 为了服务安排之目的，经营方建造或者从第三方获得的基础设施。当基础设施从属于向第三方出租人订制的融资租赁时，该基础设施应被认为是获得的基础设施。

- 为了服务安排之目的，授予方给予经营方使用权利的现有基础设施。

[IFRIC 12 第 7 段]。

部分受监管的资产

33.28　在某些特许服务权安排中，基础设施的使用部分受到授予方以上述第 33.7 段中第一个条件所述方式的监管，而部分是不受监管的。尽管这些协议可以采用不同的形式，IFRIC 12 考虑到了下述的两种情况：

- 任何物理上可分离并能独立经营以及符合 IAS 36 中现金产出单元定义的基础设施，应单独进行分析，前提是它整体出于非管制的目的被使用。例如，这可以适用于医院的私营部分，而医院的其他部分由授予方使用来医治公众病人。

- 当纯辅助性的活动（比如医院的商店）不受管制时，控制测试应视这些服务不存在而予以应用，因为在授予方以上述第 33.7 段所述的方式控制服务时，辅助性活动的存在并不影响授予方对基础设施的控制。

[IFRIC 12 para AG7].

33.29 In either of the situations described above, there may in substance be a lease from the grantor to the operator for the separable infrastructure or the facility for providing the unregulated ancillary services. If that is so, the lease should be accounted for in accordance with IAS 17. [IFRIC 12 para AG8]. The guidance in IFRIC 4 for separating payments for the lease from other payments under the arrangement would also be relevant.

Existing assets of the operator

33.30 IFRIC 12 does not apply to the operator's existing assets that are used in the service concession arrangements. The operator's existing assets include those that are used by the operator under finance leases with a third party unrelated to the grantor. The IFRIC's view is that since existing IFRSs already address rights of use and derecognition, there is no need to address the accounting treatment of the operator's existing assets that form part of the infrastructure. Thus, the operator's pre-existing infrastructure assets should continue to be recognised by the operator, unless the conditions for derecognition in IAS 16 are met. [IFRIC 12 para 8].

Example – Operator's own assets used in the arrangement

Scenario 1

The operator uses one of its assets for the whole of the concession period. The service concession arrangement, implicitly or explicitly, conveys to the grantor a right to use that asset.

In this situation, if the operator determines that this is a finance lease, the operator will derecognise the asset in accordance with IAS 17.

Scenario 2

Facts are the same as in scenario 1 except that the operator can use the asset in other projects.

In this situation, if the operator determines that this is not a lease, the operator

［IFRIC 12 AG 第 7 段］。

33.29 在上述任一情况中，实质上可能存在授予方给经营方的可分离基础设施或设备租赁，使其能够提供不受监管的辅助性服务。如果是这一情况，必须按 IAS 17 对租赁进行会计处理。［IFRIC 12 AG 第 8 段］。此外，IFRIC 4 中的指南对于将租赁款项与在该安排下的其他款项分离也具相关性。

经营方现有资产

33.30 IFRIC 12 并不适用于特许服务权安排中使用的经营方现有资产。经营方现有资产包括经营方所使用的向非关联第三方融资租入的资产。国际财务报告解释委员会的观点是由于现有的国际财务报告准则已经说明了使用权和终止确认，因而没有必要涉及经营方构成基础设施组成部分的现有资产的会计处理问题。因此，经营方业已存在的基础设施资产应继续由经营方确认，除非其满足 IAS 16 中终止确认的条件。［IFRIC 12 第 8 段］。

示例——安排中所使用的经营方自有资产

情形 1

经营方在整个特许权期间使用其一项资产。特许服务权安排默示或明确地向授予方传达使用该项资产的权利。

在此情况下，如果经营方确定此为融资租赁，经营方要根据 IAS 17 终止资产确认。

情形 2

除该经营方可以在其他项目中使用该资产以外，事实与情形 1 相同。

在此情况下，如果经营方决定这不属于租赁，经营方则要根据 IAS 16，

will continue to recognise it as property, plant and equipment in accordance with IAS 16.

Inter-relationship of IFRIC 12 with IFRSs and IFRIC 4

33.31 As explained before, IFRIC 12 does not purport to cover all public-to-private service concession arrangements, which are many and varied. Nonetheless, the IFRIC was aware of the need to consider whether broader application was appropriate for arrangements that were outside the scope of the interpretation. It felt that it would be useful to provide references to relevant standards that apply to arrangements that fall outside IFRIC 12's scope. Therefore, in order to clarify the scope of the project, the IFRIC produced a table of references to relevant standards for the types of arrangements considered by the interpretation.

33.32 The table below sets out various types of private arrangements for the provision of public service that are typical, but not exhaustive. It provides a valuable roadmap, pointing concession operators to the relevant IFRSs and helping them apply those IFRSs to service concession arrangements. IFRIC 12 applies to arrangements in the shaded area where the application of IFRSs is most unclear. The purpose of the table is to highlight the continuum of arrangements, not to convey the impression that 'bright lines' exist between arrangements or between the accounting requirements.

继续将其确认其为不动产、工厂和设备。

IFRIC 12 与国际财务报告准则和 IFRIC 4 之间的关系

33.31 正如之前的解释，IFRIC 12 无意涵盖所有的公共 - 私营特许服务权安排。尽管如此，国际财务报告解释委员会知道其需要考虑更广泛地将其应用于解释范围以外的安排是否合适。它觉得为 IFRIC 12 范围以外的安排提供相关准则的参照将会有用。因此，为了明确项目的范围，国际财务报告解释委员会针对该解释所涉及的安排类型制作了一份相关准则的参照图表。

33.32 下表列出了私营部门参与提供公共服务的安排的典型类型，但协议类型的列示并未穷尽。它提供了一个有用的路标，引导特许权经营方了解相关的国际财务报告准则，并帮助他们将这些国际财务报告准则应用于特许服务权安排。IFRIC 12 应用于下表中阴影部分，这些安排是《国际财务报告准则》应用中最不明晰的。该表的目的是为了突出安排之间的连续统一性，而不想传达各项安排之间或其会计处理要求之间存在鲜明界限的印象。

References to IFRSs that apply to typical types of public-to-private arrangements

Category	Lessee	Service provider			Owner	
Typical arrangement types	Lease (for example, operator leases asset from grantor)	Service and/or maintenance contract (specific tasks for example, debt collection)	Rehabilitate-operate-transfer	Build-operate-transfer	Build-own-operate	100% Divestment/privatisation/corporation
Asset ownership	Grantor				Operator	
Capital investment	Grantor		Grantor		Operator	
Demand risk	Shared	Grantor	Operator and/or grantor		Operator	
Typical duration	8 – 20 years	1 – 5 years	25 – 30 year			Indefinite (or may be limited by licence)
Residual interest	Grantor				Operator	
Relevant IFRSs	IAS 17	IAS 18	IFRIC 12		IAS 16	

[IFRIC 12 – Information note 2].

33.33 IFRIC 12 identifies types of arrangements that may be very similar to leases. Consequently, it may be difficult in practice to decide whether such an arrangement would fall to be accounted for under IFRIC 4/IAS 17, which gives the operator 'a right to control the use of an asset' or, under IFRIC 12, which gives the operator 'a right of access' while the grantor retains 'control of the right to use the asset'. Clearly, such a choice could lead to different accounting treatments for arrangements that have similar economic effects, which was not the intention of the IFRIC. Accordingly, the IFRIC amended IFRIC 4's scope to specify that if a

适用于公共－私营安排典型类型的国际财务报告准则参考

<table>
<tr><th>类别</th><th>承租人</th><th colspan="3">服务提供方</th><th colspan="2">所有者</th></tr>
<tr><td>典型安排类别</td><td>租赁（例如经营方从授予方租赁资产）</td><td>服务和/或维护合同（特定任务，例如讨债）</td><td>复原－经营－转移</td><td>建造－经营－转移</td><td>建造－拥有－经营</td><td>100%出售/私有化/公司</td></tr>
<tr><td>资产所有权</td><td colspan="2">授予方</td><td colspan="2"></td><td colspan="2">经营方</td></tr>
<tr><td>资本投资</td><td colspan="2">授予方</td><td colspan="2">授予方</td><td colspan="2">经营方</td></tr>
<tr><td>需求风险</td><td>共担</td><td>授予方</td><td colspan="2">经营方和/或授予方</td><td colspan="2">经营方</td></tr>
<tr><td>典型期间</td><td>8—20 年</td><td>1—5 年</td><td colspan="2">25—30 年</td><td></td><td>不确定（或者可以以许可权限定）</td></tr>
<tr><td>剩余权益</td><td colspan="2">授予方</td><td colspan="2"></td><td colspan="2">经营方</td></tr>
<tr><td>相关国际财务报告准则</td><td>IAS 17</td><td>IAS 18</td><td colspan="2">IFRIC 12</td><td colspan="2">IAS 16</td></tr>
</table>

[IFRIC 12——信息附注 2]。

33.33　IFRIC 12 辨认出可能与租赁非常类似的安排类型。因而，实务中可能很难决定此类安排是否应按照 IFRIC 4/IAS 17 进行会计处理；IFRIC 4/IAS 17 赋予经营方"控制资产使用的权利"，或者 IFRIC 12 赋予经营方"使用权"而授予方保留"对资产使用权的控制"。很明显，这样的选择可能导致对于具有相似经济效应的安排进行不同的会计处理，而这并非国际财务报告解释委员会的初衷。因此，国际财务报告解释委员会修改了 IFRIC 4 的范围，明确符合 IFRIC 12 范围要求的特许服务权安排将不属于 IFRIC 4 的范围。

service arrangement met IFRIC 12's scope requirements it would not be within IFRIC 4's scope.

Private-to-private arrangements

33. 34 IFRIC 12 is limited to arrangements involving infrastructure service concessions – the most significant characteristics of which is that the grantor controls the right to use the infrastructure or its output available to the public because of the nature of the public services provided, irrespective of who operates it. Normally, the grantor will be a public body or a private sector entity to which the responsibility for the service has been devolved. [IFRIC 12 para 3(a)]. However, there is nothing in IFRIC 12 to suggest that this must always be so. The grantor itself can be a private sector body that has a public service obligation and can enter into a service concession arrangement with a private sector operator. Although such arrangements may be few and far between, they will fall within IFRIC 12's scope.

33. 35 In addition, the IFRIC noted that IFRIC 12's scope may be extended to private-to-private arrangements by analogy under the hierarchy set out in paragraphs 7 to 12 of IAS 8 when no standards or interpretations apply directly. This may be appropriate in circumstances where the arrangement meets similar requirements to those specified in IFRIC 12, that is:

- the arrangement meets the requirements for control by the grantor set out in paragraph 33. 7 above; and
- the arrangement embodies a public service obligation as described in paragraph 33. 9 above.

[IFRIC 12 para BC14].

Accounting for service concession arrangements

Introduction

33. 36 As explained in paragraph 33. 7 above, IFRIC 12's scope is limited to the

私营——私营安排

33.34　IFRIC 12 仅限于涉及基础设施特许服务权的安排——此类安排最为重要的特征是授予方控制基础设施的使用权，或者因为其所提供的公共服务的性质，其产出要对公众开放，而无论谁为经营方。一般而言，授予方将是公共实体或是负责已被移交的服务的私营部门实体。[IFRIC 12 第 3（a）段]。然而，IFRIC 12 未表明必须一贯如此。授予方本身可以是负有公共服务义务的私营部门实体，并能与私营部门经营方签订特许服务权安排。尽管此类协议可能较少见，但其属于 IFRIC 12 的范围。

33.35　另外，国际财务报告解释委员会指出，在没有准则或解释可直接应用的情况下，在 IAS 8 第 7 段至第 12 段所设定的级次之下，通过类推，IFRIC 12 的适用范围可能被推及私营－私营安排。在安排符合 IFRIC 12 所规定的如下类似要求时，这可能适用：

■ 安排符合如上述第 33.7 段所陈述的授予方控制要求；以及

■ 如上述第 33.9 段所述，安排体现公共服务义务。

[IFRIC 12 BC 第 14 段]。

特许服务权安排的会计处理

引言

33.36　如上第 33.7 段中的解释，IFRIC 12 的范围仅限于受控于授予方的公

accounting by operators for public-to private service concession arrangements that are controlled by the grantor. The operator acts as a service provider. The operator constructs or upgrades infrastructure (construction or upgrade services) used to provide a public service and operates and maintains that infrastructure (operation services) for a specified period. Therefore, for accounting purposes, it is first necessary to determine the nature of the operator's rights over the infrastructure that it constructs or upgrades.

Nature of operator's rights over the infrastructure

33.37 Infrastructure within IFRIC 12's scope should not be recognised as property, plant and equipment of the operator because the contractual service arrangement does not convey the right to control the infrastructure to the operator. The operator has access to operate the infrastructure to provide the public service on the grantor's behalf in accordance with the contract's terms [IFRIC 12 para 11]. This applies whether the infrastructure is constructed or acquired by the operator or is provided by the grantor for the purposes of the concession.

33.38 Control should be distinguished from management. If the grantor retains both the degree of control described in the first point in paragraph 33.7 above and any significant residual interest in the infrastructure, the operator is only managing the infrastructure on the grantor's behalf – even though, in many instances, it may have wide managerial discretion. [IFRIC 12 para AG5].

Control versus risks and rewards

33.39 The above requirement is based on the notion of control. Under IFRIC 12, where an operator constructs or acquires an infrastructure asset or is given access to it by the grantor for the provision of a public service, the recognition of the infrastructure asset by the operator is based solely on the basis of 'control of use' and not on the extent to which the operator or the grantor bears the 'risk and rewards of ownership'. This is a key feature of IFRIC 12, which determines the scope and the applicability of other standards and interpretations to service concession arrangements. This aspect of control, which is separate from

共—私营特许服务权安排的经营方会计处理。经营方作为服务提供商。经营方建造或改良（建造或改良服务）用于提供公共服务的基础设施，并在规定的期间经营和维护该基础设施（经营服务）。因此，出于会计处理的目的，首先必须确定经营方对于其所建造或改良的基础设施所拥有的权利的性质。

经营方对于基础设施所拥有的权利的性质

33.37　IFRIC 12 范围内的基础设施不应该被确认为经营方的不动产、工厂和设备，因为合同服务协议并未向经营方让渡基础设施的控制权。经营方系依据合同条款代表授予方经营基础设施，以提供公共服务［IFRIC 12 第 11 段］。无论基础设施是由经营方建造或购买，或是由授予方出于特许权之目的而提供，其均适用。

33.38　控制必须区别于管理。如果授予方既保留上述第 33.7 段中第一点所述的控制程度，又保留基础设施的任何重大剩余权益，那么经营方只是代表授予方管理基础设施——尽管在许多情况下，其可能拥有广泛的自主管理权。［IFRIC 12 AG 第 5 段］。

控制对风险和报酬

33.39　以上要求以控制概念为基础。根据 IFRIC 12，当经营方建造或者购买基础设施资产，或者被授予方允许使用基础设施以提供公共服务的情况下，经营方对基础设施资产的确认仅仅是基于“使用控制”的基本原则，而非基于经营方或者授予方承担“所有权风险和报酬”的程度。这是 IFRIC 12 的主要特征，决定了其他准则和解释对特许服务权安排的范围和适用性。控制的这一层面，是从所有权中分离出来的，也是 IFRIC 12 区别于以前经营方所应用的其他国家一般公认会计准则之处。

ownership, also distinguishes IFRIC 12 from other national GAAPs that have previously been applied by operators.

33.40 In arriving at the above requirement, the IFRIC first examined whether the infrastructure could be recognised by the operator under IAS 16. It concluded that the control of the right to use an asset as defined in the Framework – a resource controlled by the entity as a result of past event and from which future economic benefits are expected to flow – determines recognition under IAS 16 for items that are 'held for use'. Given that it is the grantor who controls the use of the infrastructure in the manner described in paragraph 33.7 above, the operator would not be in a position to control the use of the infrastructure and should therefore not recognise the infrastructure as its property, plant and equipment under IAS 16, regardless of which party has legal title.

33.41 In other words, in arrangements falling within IFRIC 12's scope, the operator acts as a service provider. The operator constructs or upgrades infrastructure used to provide a public service. Under the contract's terms the operator has access to operate the infrastructure to provide the public service on the grantor's behalf. The asset recognised by the operator is the consideration it receives in exchange for its services, not the public service infrastructure that it constructs or upgrades. [IFRIC 12 para BC25].

33.42 The IFRIC also considered whether arrangements within IFRIC 12's scope convey 'the right to control the use of the public service infrastructure'. The IFRIC concluded that if an arrangement meets the control conditions in paragraph 33.7 above, the operator would not have the right to control the use of the infrastructure and should, therefore, not recognise the infrastructure as a leased asset. [IFRIC 12 paras BC22 – BC23].

33.43 In other words, for arrangements within IFRIC 12's scope, the operator's right is different from that of a lessee. The grantor retains control over the use to which the infrastructure is put and retains control over any significant residual interest in the infrastructure throughout the period of the arrangement. This both restricts the operator's practical ability to sell or pledge the infrastructure and gives the grantor a continuing right of use. Consequently, unlike a lessee, the operator does not have a genuine right to use the infrastructure. Rather, it has access to

33.40 为达成上述要求，国际财务报告解释委员会首先审查经营方是否可以根据 IAS 16 对基础设施进行确认。其结论是，框架中所定义的对资产使用权的控制（由过去事项形成的、由企业控制的、并预期未来会给企业带来经济利益流入的资源）决定了“持有以供使用”的项目在 IAS 16 下的确认。如果授予方按上述第 33.7 段所述方式控制基础设施的使用，则经营方不能控制基础设施的使用，那么依据 IAS 16，无论何方拥有合法所有权，经营方不应将基础设施作为其不动产、工厂和设备进行确认。

33.41 换言之，在属于 IFRIC 12 范围的安排中，经营方担任服务提供者。经营方建造或改良基础设施，用于提供公共服务。根据合同条款，经营方有权代表授予方运营基础设施，以提供公共服务。经营方确认的资产是其提供服务交换所得对价，而非其建设或改良的公共服务基础设施。[IFRIC 12 BC 第 25 段]。

33.42 国际财务报告解释委员会也在考虑，属于 IFRIC 12 范围的安排是否传达了“公共服务基础设施使用控制权”的意思。国际财务报告解释委员会的结论是，如果安排满足上述第 33.7 段中的控制条件，则经营方无权控制基础设施的使用，因而不应将基础设施确认为租赁资产。[IFRIC 12 BC 第 22—23 段]。

33.43 换言之，对于属于 IFRIC 12 范围的安排，经营方的权利不同于承租人。授予方在整个协议期内，保留基础设施使用的控制权，并保留基础设施任何重大剩余权益的控制权。这两个方面实际上都在制约着经营方出售或抵押基础设施的能力，并赋予授予方继续使用的权利。因而，不同于承租人，经营方对基础设施没有真正的使用权。相反，经营方系根据合同规定的条款代表授予方经营基础设施，以提供公共服务。[IFRIC 12 BC 第 28 段]。

operate the infrastructure to provide the public service on behalf of the grantor in accordance with the terms specified in the contract. [IFRIC 12 para BC 28].

Example – Control versus risk and rewards

The terms of a service concession arrangement require a private sector operator to finance, build, maintain and operate a toll bridge. The government sets the toll and controls the residual interest in the bridge. The operator bears the construction risk (cost and time overruns during the construction period), changes in costs relating to maintenance and demand risk associated with the usage of the toll bridge.

In this situation, even though the operator constructs the toll bridge using its own funds and bears significant cost risks and variations in revenue from tolls collected, it cannot recognise the bridge as its property, plant and equipment. This is because, in accordance with paragraph 33.7 above, it is the grantor not the operator that controls the use of the toll bridge.

Recognition of consideration given by the grantor to the operator

33.44 Given that the operator is neither permitted to recognise the infrastructure nor a lease of the infrastructure, the asset the operator recognises is the consideration it receives from the grantor in exchange for providing construction or upgrade services. The consideration received can take a variety of forms. The different rights to receive consideration are not necessarily rights to receive cash or other financial assets. The consideration given by the grantor to the operator may be rights to:

- a financial asset; or
- an intangible asset.

[IFRIC 12 para 15].

33.45 Sometimes part of the consideration can be in the form of a tangible asset, such as land (see further para 33.119). The nature of the consideration given by

示例——控制对风险和报酬

特许服务权安排的条款要求经营方融资、修建、维护并经营一座收费桥梁。政府制定收费标准并控制桥梁的剩余权益。经营方承担建造风险（建造期间费用超支和工期延误）、与维护有关的成本变化以及与收费桥梁使用有关的需求风险。

在此情况下，尽管经营方使用其自有资金建造该收费桥梁并承担重大成本风险以及来自所收费用收入变化之风险，其不能将桥梁确认为不动产、工厂和设备。这是因为，依据上述第 33. 7 段，是授予方而非经营方控制着收费桥梁的使用。

授予方给予经营方对价的确认

33. 44　由于经营方既没有被允许确认基础设施，也没有被允许确认对基础设施的租赁，经营方确认的资产是其提供建造或改良服务，从授予方所得的对价。所获得的对价可以采取多种形式。获得对价的权利并不一定是取得现金或者其他金融资产的权利。授予方给予经营方的对价可能是如下权利：

- 金融资产，或
- 无形资产。

［IFRIC 12 第 15 段］。

33. 45　有时部分对价可以是有形资产的形式，如土地（参见下文第 33. 119 段）。授予方给予经营方的对价的性质应参照合同条款，且如果存在相关合同

the grantor to the operator should be determined by reference to the contract terms and, when it exists, relevant contract law. [IFRIC 12 para 19]. Whatever form the consideration takes, it should be measured at its fair value. [IFRIC 12 para 15].

33.46 Furthermore, the grantor does not need to pay the cash to the operator directly. The users may pay the contractual amount directly to the operator at the grantor's direction. The method of payment is a matter of form only and does not alter the nature of the operator's asset, whether it is financial or intangible asset. In other words, the payee's identity has no effect on the risks to the operator's cash flows. The operator typically relies on the service concession arrangement's terms to determine the risks to its cash flow streams.

Operator recognises a financial asset

33.47 The operator should recognise a financial asset to the extent that it has an unconditional contractual right to receive cash or another financial asset from, or at the direction of, the grantor for the construction services. This is consistent with the definition of financial asset in IAS 32. [IAS 32 para 11]. In other words, the operator recognises a financial asset if the grantor has little or no discretion to avoid payment. This is usually because the agreement is enforceable by law. [IFRIC 12 para 16; IAS 32 para 13]. For example, the service concession arrangement may require the operator to construct a road or a hospital for which it receives a right to be paid by the grantor. The operator recognises a financial asset representing its accumulating right to be paid for providing construction services during the construction phase (see further para 33.82).

Specified or determinable amounts

33.48 In some service concession arrangements, the operator may have a contractual right to receive specified or determinable payments from the grantor. [IFRIC 12 para 16]. Either users or grantors may pay the contractual amount receivable directly to the operator. As explained in the paragraph 33.46 above, the nature of the operator's asset is not altered solely because the contractual amount

法规的话，应一并参照。[IFRIC 12 第 19 段]。无论对价采用何种形式，均应以公允价值计量。[IFRIC 12 第 15 段]。

33.46　此外，授予方无需直接向经营方支付现金。使用者可以在授予方的指示下，直接向经营方支付合同金额。付款方式仅仅是形式问题，并不改变经营方资产的性质，无论其为金融资产或无形资产。换言之，收款人的身份对于经营方现金流量的风险没有影响。经营方通常根据特许服务权安排的条款确定其现金流量的风险。

经营方确认金融资产

33.47　经营方针对其建造服务，在有无条件合同权利从授予方处，或按照授予方的指示，取得现金或其它金融资产的权利的限度内，确认一项金融资产。这与 IAS 32 中的金融资产定义相一致。[IAS 32 第 11 段]。换言之，如果授予方没有或几乎没有回避付款的自由裁量权，则经营方确认金融资产。这通常是因为协议具有法律强制执行力。[IFRIC 12 第 16 段；IAS 32 第 13 段]。例如，特许服务权安排可能要求经营方修建道路或医院，以取得从授予方获得付款的权利。经营方确认一项金融资产，代表其在建造阶段提供建造服务而累积的收款权利（参见下文第 33.82 段）。

规定或者可确定的金额

33.48　在一些特许服务权安排中，经营方可能拥有从授予方处获得规定的或可确定的付款的合同权利。[IFRIC 12 第 16 段]。使用者或授予方会直接向经营方支付合同应收金额。如上述第 33.46 段中的解释，经营方资产的性质不会仅仅因为合同应收金额可能由公共服务使用者直接支付而发生改变。

receivable may be paid directly by users of the public service.

Example – Specified payments from the grantor

The terms of a service concession arrangement require a private sector operator to finance, build, maintain and operate a prison for 20 years. The grantor pays the operator an annual sum per year that increases in line with inflation.

In this situation, the operator has a contractual right to receive a specified or determinable amount of cash from the grantor, irrespective of whether the prison is partially or fully occupied. The operator recognises a financial asset.

Operator's cash flows are contingent on performance or availability

33.49 In many service concession arrangements, the operator may have to fulfil performance obligations before it can exercise its rights to receive payments from the grantor. For example, the operator may have to construct the infrastructure to a specified quality or ensure that the infrastructure meets operating or efficiency targets so that a specified level of service or capacity may be delivered to the public. Failure to meet the specified quality, performance or efficiency target may result in the operator incurring penalties for under-performance.

33.50 In such situations, the operator recognises a financial asset even though its right to receive cash is contingent on meeting specified requirements. [IFRIC 12 para 16]. In other words, the variation in cash flows due to under-performance would not prevent the amount of the consideration to be received from the grantor being 'determinable'. Furthermore, IAS 32 provides evidence that such contingent rights meet the definition of a financial asset. It states that '*the ability to exercise a contractual right or the requirement to satisfy a contractual obligation may be absolute, or it may be contingent on the occurrence of a future event*'. [IAS 32 para AG8].

33.51 Variation in cash flows may also occur where payments are made by the grantor only if the infrastructure is 'available' for use. For example, in a road infrastructure contract, no payment is made by the grantor if certain lanes are closed for more than a minimal period. Any penalties or reductions in payments for

示例——由授予方规定的付款

特许服务权安排的条款要求私营部门经营方融资、建造、维护和运营一座监狱长达20年。授予方每年向经营方支付一笔年费，与通货膨胀同步增长。

在此情况下，经营方拥有从授予方处收取规定的或者是可确定金额现金的合同权利，无论该监狱是部分还是全部投入使用。经营方确认一项金融资产。

经营方的现金流量取决于业绩或可用性

33.49　在许多特许服务权安排中，经营方可能必须要完成业绩任务，才能够行使从授予方处获得付款的权利。例如，经营方可能一定要按规定的质量建造基础设施，或者确保基础设施符合运营或效率目标，以便能向公众提供规定水平的服务或功能。未符合规定的质量、业绩或者效率目标可能导致经营方因表现欠佳而受到处罚。

33.50　在此情况下，经营方仍确认一项金融资产，尽管其获得现金的权利取决于是否符合规定的要求。[IFRIC 12 第16段]。换言之，由于业绩欠佳而导致现金流量变化并不妨碍从授予方处获得“可确定的”对价金额。此外，IAS 32 为此类或有权利符合金融资产的定义提供了证据。IAS 32 指出，“*行使合同权利的能力或履行合同义务的要求可能是无条件的，也可能取决于某一未来事项的出现*”。[IAS 32 AG 第8段]。

33.51　如果只有在基础设施“可供”使用的情况下授予方才付款，现金流量也可能发生变化。例如，在道路基础设施合同中，如果某些车道关闭超过某段最低期限，则授予方不会付款。对于不可用性的任何罚款或者扣款与不动产是否处于可用状态有关，而并不反映需求风险的存在（参见下述第33.53

non-availability relate to whether the property is in a state fit for use and do not reflect the existence of demand risk (see para 33. 53 below) or the grantor's commitment to pay. Therefore, consistent with the above discussion, the operator recognises a financial asset even though its right to receive cash is based solely on availability.

Shortfall in user payments guaranteed by grantor

33. 52 In some service concession arrangements, the grantor may guarantee to pay the operator the shortfall, if any, between amounts received from users of the public service and specified or determinable amounts. In this situation, the operator has an unconditional right to receive the minimum guaranteed amount that the grantor cannot avoid. Consequently, the operator recognises a financial asset for the full amount of the cash guaranteed by the grantor.

Example – Shortfall guaranteed by the grantor

The terms of a service concession arrangement require a private sector operator to finance, build, maintain and operate a toll road for 20 years. The operator forecasts that revenue from tolls is expected to be approximately C10m a year based on a constant level of traffic for the whole of the concession period. This amount is expected to be sufficient to enable the operator to recover its investment in the infrastructure and earn a return. However, if cash flows fall short of expectation, the grantor guarantees to pay the operator any shortfall between C10m per year and the actual tolls collected. Any excess of C10m is retained by the operator.

In this situation, the guarantee has the effect that the grantor controls the total minimum amount and has no discretion to avoid making such payments to the operator. The grantor's liability is reduced by amounts received by the operator directly from users and may result in no payment under the guarantee. Nevertheless, the operator has an unconditional right to receive cash of C10m per year as consideration for building the road from or at the direction of the grantor, irrespective of usage levels. Thus, the operator recognises a financial asset representing its right to receive a fixed monetary

段），或授予方的支付承诺。因而，与上述讨论相一致，经营方确认一项金融资产，尽管其获取现金的权利仅基于可用性。

由授予方担保的使用者付款差额

33.52 在一些特许服务权安排中，如果从公共服务使用者处收取的金额与规定或可确定的金额之间存在差额，授予方可能向经营者担保支付上述差额。在此情况下，经营方拥有无条件获得最低担保金额的权利，而授予方无法回避这一情况。所以，经营方以授予方所担保现金全额确认一项金融资产。

示例——授予方担保的差额

特许服务权安排的条款要求某私营部门经营方融资、建造、维护和运营一条收费公路20年。经营方基于整个特许期间一个恒定的交通量，预计来自通行费的收入每年约为1,000万元。预计这一金额足以使经营方收回其在基础设施中的投资并获得回报。然而，如果收入低于预期，授予方担保向经营方每年支付1,000万元与实际收取的通行费之间的任何差额。任何超过1,000万元的金额将由经营方保留。

在此情况下，担保具有使授予方控制全部最低金额，而且没有对经营方回避支付这一款项的自由裁量权的作用。授予方的债务随经营方直接从使用者处收到的金额而减少，并可能导致无需支付任何款项，尽管授予方承诺支付差额。然而，经营方拥有每年无条件获得1,000万元现金的权利，作为按授予方指示或从授予方处获得的修建公路的对价，与使用程度无关。因此，经营方确认一项金融资产，代表其每年有获得1,000万元固定货币金额的权利。

amount of C10m per year.

Demand risk

33.53 Demand risk is risk that the demand or usage for the infrastructure asset will be greater or less than expected. Service concession arrangements are typically for long periods and create greater demand risk, because of the uncertainties concerning the extent to which the public will use the infrastructure asset in the future. The terms of the arrangement would indicate whether demand risk is borne by the grantor, or the operator, or whether it is shared between the two parties.

33.54 The example in paragraph 33.52 demonstrates that the operator has an unconditional right to receive cash to the extent that the grantor bears the risk that the cash flows generated by the users of the public service will not be sufficient to recover the operator's investment. That is, where the grantor bears the demand risk, the operator's cash flows are not dependent on the usage of the infrastructure. The operator's cash flows are effectively secured, which results in a financial asset as consideration received for its construction services. That is, where a service concession arrangement is subject to a grantor guarantee, payments made by users are effectively regarded as cash collected on behalf of the grantor and give rise to a financial asset for the commitment made by the grantor.

33.55 In contrast, if the operator's cash flows are dependent on the usage of the infrastructure, the operator bears demand risk. This is the case in the above example where the operator is exposed to risk in excess of the guaranteed amount. In that situation, the nature of the asset recognised is different and this is considered below.

Operator recognises an intangible asset

33.56 In some service concession arrangements, like the one illustrated in the example in paragraph 33.48 above, users pay for the services provided by the operator and the operator recovers its investments in the infrastructure from the payments made by the users. In the absence of any contractual arrangement designed to ensure that the operator receives a specified minimum return, such as a

需求风险

33.53　需求风险是基础设施资产的需求或使用高于或低于预期的风险。特许服务权安排通常周期较长，由于涉及公众将来使用基础设施资产程度的不确定性，因而产生较大的需求风险。安排条款会说明，需求风险是由授予方还是经营方来承担，或者由两者共担。

33.54　上述第33.52段中的示例显示，在授予方承担公共服务使用者所产生的现金流量不足以抵补经营方投资这一风险的情况下，经营方拥有无条件获得现金的权利。即在授予方承担需求风险的情况下，经营方的现金流量并不取决于基础设施的使用情况。经营方的现金流量得到有效保证，因而产生了一项金融资产，作为其建造服务所获得的对价。换言之，在特许服务权安排从属于授予方担保的情况下，使用者支付的款项实际上是看作代表授予方筹集的现金，产生反映授予方承诺的金融资产。

33.55　相比之下，如果经营方的现金流量取决于基础设施的使用情况，那么则由经营方承担需求风险。上例中经营方承担超出担保金额的风险便属于这种情况。在那种情况下，所确认的资产的性质是不同的，而这是下面要考虑的问题。

经营方确认无形资产

33.56　在一些特许服务权安排中，如上述第33.48段中的示例说明的安排，使用者为经营方提供的服务支付款项，而经营方则通过使用者支付的款项收回其在基础设施中的投资。在无任何旨在确保经营方收取特定最低回报的合同安排（如上述所考虑的差额担保）的情况下，经营方无从任何其他方获得现金的合同权利，即使收取现金的可能性非常大。相反，经营方有机会向将

shortfall guarantee considered above, the operator has no contractual right to receive cash from any other party, even if receipt of cash is highly probable. Rather, the operator has an opportunity to charge users who choose to use the infrastructure in the future.

33.57 The IFRIC takes the view that since the operator cannot recognise the infrastructure as its own, the operator's right to charge users meets the definition of an intangible asset that should be accounted for in accordance with IAS 38. The view taken by IFRIC is that the operator receives an intangible right to charge users in exchange for its construction services. It is, in effect, akin to a licence.

33.58 Accordingly, the operator should recognise an intangible asset to the extent that it receives a right (a licence) to charge users of the public service. A right to charge users of the public service is not an unconditional right to receive cash, because the amounts are contingent on the extent that the public uses the service. [IFRIC 12 para 17].

Example – Operator's revenue is conditional on usage

A service concession arrangement's terms require a private sector operator to finance, build, maintain and operate a toll road for 20 years. The operator receives tolls from users based on usage. There are no shortfall guarantees in place.

In this case, the grantor gives the operator the right to charge users for using the road. As the operator's cash flows are contingent on users using the public service, the operator bears demand risk. Therefore, the operator recognises an intangible asset for the construction services.

The answer would be the same if the grantor, rather than the users, paid the operator based on usage. Such arrangements are often described as 'shadow tolls'. In this situation, the operator does not have an unconditional right to receive cash as the amounts are contingent on usage. Accordingly, the operator recognises an intangible asset. As explained in paragraph 33.46 above, the identity of the party that makes the payments does not affect the classification.

来选择使用基础设施的使用者收费。

33.57　国际财务报告解释委员会认为，由于经营方无法将基础设施确认为自身资产，经营方向使用者收费的权利符合无形资产的定义，应按照IAS 38处理。国际财务报告解释委员会所持的观点是，经营方获得向使用者收费的无形权利，用以交换其建造服务。事实上这类似于一种许可。

33.58　相应地，经营方在其获得向公共服务使用者收费的权利（许可）的情况下，应当确认无形资产。向公共服务使用者收费的权利不是无条件获得现金的权利，因为其金额取决于公众使用服务的程度。[IFRIC 12 第17段]。

示例——经营方的收入取决于使用情况

特许服务权安排的条款要求私营部门经营方融资、建造、维护和运营一条收费公路长达20年。经营方基于使用情况向使用者收取通行费。此安排无差额担保。

在此情况下，授予方赋予经营方向道路使用者收费的权利。由于经营方的现金流量取决于使用者对公共服务的使用情况，经营方承担了需求风险。因此，经营方将建造服务确认为无形资产。

如果是授予方，而不是使用者，基于使用情况向经营方付款，答案是一样的。这样的协议常常被描述为“影子收费”。在此情况下，经营方没有无条件获取现金的权利，因为其金额取决于使用情况。相应地，经营方确认无形资产。如上述第33.46段中的解释，付款方的身份并不影响分类。

Operator receives a substantially fixed return

33. 59 In some concession arrangements the operator may receive amounts from the users but, rather than receiving any shortfall guaranteed by the grantor, the price charged by the operator is varied by regulation designed to ensure that the operator receives a substantially fixed return. In other service concession arrangements, the operator may be permitted to collect revenues from users until it achieved a specified return on its investment in the public service infrastructure asset, at which point the concession comes to an end and the infrastructure reverts back to the grantor.

33. 60 Arrangements of the type described above have the effect of eliminating substantially all the variations in operator's return. However, such arrangements will still be recognised as intangible assets because the operator does not have the contractual right to receive cash. The fact that the operator's return is low risk and, therefore, it is highly likely to obtain its specified return does not change the fact that the operator has no contractual right to collect revenues from users or grantor.

Operator recognises both a financial asset and an intangible asset

33. 61 As discussed above, the nature of the asset recognised by the operator depends on the allocation of demand risk and not on the quantum of the risk. At one extreme, all, or substantially all, of the demand risk may be borne by the grantor giving rise to a financial asset. At the other extreme, all or substantially all, of the demand risk may be borne by the operator giving rise to an intangible asset. In between, there may be arrangements where the demand risk is shared between the grantor and the operator.

33. 62 Consider the example in paragraph 33. 52 above, where the operator collects tolls from users but the grantor provides a shortfall guarantee that the operator's return will not fall below a specified minimum. In that situation, the risk (demand risk) is shared between the grantor and the operator such that the cash flows generated by users of the public service may not be sufficient to recover the

经营方获得实质上固定的回报

33.59　在一些特许服务权安排中，经营方可能从使用者那里收费，而不是取得授予方担保的任何差额，但经营方收费的价格随监管而变化，旨在确保经营方获取实质上固定的回报。在其他特许服务权安排中，经营方可能被允许从使用者处取得收入，直到达成其在公共服务基础设施资产投资中规定的回报，在此时点特许权协议结束，而基础设施归还给授予方。

33.60　上述类型的协议具有实质上消除经营方回报中所有变化的作用。不过，此类协议仍将被确认为无形资产，因为经营方并没有获得现金的合同权利。经营方回报是低风险的，因而其很可能获得规定回报的事实，并没有改变经营方没有从使用者或者授予方处获得收入的合同权利的事实。

经营方既确认金融资产又确认无形资产

33.61　如上面所讨论，经营方所确认的资产的性质取决于需求风险的分配，而不是风险的总量。在一个极端情况下，授予方可能承担所有的、或者实质上所有的需求风险，这样便产生一项金融资产。在另一个极端情况下，经营方可能承担所有的、或者实质上所有的需求风险，这样便产生一项无形资产。在两者之间，也许存在需求风险由授予方和经营方共担的协议。

33.62　考虑一下上述第 33.52 段中的示例，经营方从使用者处收取通行费，但授予方提供差额担保使经营方的回报不会低于规定的最低限额。在此情况下，风险（需求风险）由授予方和经营方共担，而公共服务使用者所产生的现金流量可能不足以收回经营方的投资。授予方承担差额担保，而经营方承担需求风险，即超过最低限额的部分。国际财务报告解释委员会的结论是，

operator's investment. The grantor bears the shortfall guarantee and the operator bears demand risk, that is, upside, in excess of the minimum guarantee. The IFRIC concluded that in these circumstances it would be necessary to divide the operator's consideration into a financial asset component for any guaranteed amount of cash or other financial asset as already discussed in paragraph 33. 52 above, and an intangible asset for the remainder. The intangible asset in this situation gives the operator the right to earn amounts from users in excess of the minimum. [IFRIC 12 para BC53].

33. 63 Accordingly, where the operator is paid for the construction services partly by a financial asset and partly by an intangible asset, it is necessary to account separately for each component of the operator's consideration. The consideration for both components should be recognised initially at the fair value of the consideration received or receivable. [IFRIC 12 para 18]. In practice, this type of concession arrangement, where the operator and the grantor share demand risk giving rise to a financial as well as an intangible asset, is likely to be fairly common. Therefore, it would be necessary to look carefully at the terms of the public-to-private sector agreement and exercise judgement to determine the true nature of the consideration received by the operator.

33. 64 The way in which the incidence of demand risk between the grantor and the operator affects the nature of the asset recognised by the operator is shown in the table below for various service concession arrangements.

Table showing incidence of demand risk for various payment structures and the nature of the asset recognised by the operator

		Nature of infrastructure asset recognised by the operator	
Para ref	**Payment structure**	**Financial**	**Intangible**
33. 48 above	Grantor pays operator specific or determinable payments and bears demand risk	√	
33. 49	Grantor pays operator variable amounts contingent on performance or availability	√	

在这些情况下，有必要将经营方的对价就任何现金或其他金额资产的担保金额，如上述第33.52段已讨论的划分为金融资产组成部分，并将其余部分划分为无形资产。在此情况下的无形资产给予经营方从使用者处赚取超过最低限额的权利。[IFRIC 12BC第53段]。

33.63　因此，在经营方因建造服务而收到付款，其中部分付款为金融资产、部分付款为无形资产的情况下，有必要对经营方对价的每个组成部分分别进行会计处理。两个组成部分的对价必须以所获得或应获得的对价的公允价值进行初始确认。[IFRIC 12第18段]。在实务中，此类经营方和授予方共担需求风险并产生金融资产和无形资产的特许权安排很可能是相当普遍的。因此，有必要仔细审阅公共－私营部门安排的条款，并判断以确定经营方所获得的对价的性质。

33.64　对于各种不同的特许服务权安排，需求风险在授予方和经营方之间的影响范围影响经营方所确认资产的性质的方式如以下图表所示。

展示各类付款结构的需求风险的影响范围和经营方所确认的资产性质的图表

		经营方所确认基础设施资产的性质	
参考段落	**付款结构**	**金融资产**	**无形资产**
上述第33.48段	授予方向经营方支付规定的或可确定的付款，并承担需求风险。	√	
第33.49段	授予方根据业绩或可用性，向经营方支付金额不等的款项。	√	

con.

		Nature of infrastructure asset recognised by the operator	
Para ref	**Payment structure**	**Financial**	**Intangible**
33. 58	Users pay operator based on usage and operator bears demand risk		√
33. 58	Grantor pays operator based on usage and operator bears demand risk		√
33. 59	Users pay operator but price charged is varied by regulator to ensure that operator receives a substantially fixed return. Operator bears demand risk even if that risk is low		√
33. 59	Users pay operator and concession continues until operator has achieved its return on investments. Operator bears demand risk through the concession period.		√
33. 62	Users pay operator based on usage, but grantor guarantees that payments will not fall below a specified minimum (shortfall guarantee). Demand risk shared between grantor and operator.	√ (minimum due from grantor)	√ (excess over minimum due from users)

It should be noted that any recognition of a financial asset or an intangible asset implies that the operator has provided construction or upgrade services to the grantor. No asset arises where the arrangement does not involve any construction or upgrade services and there is no obligation to pay the grantor or third party (see further para 33. 102 below).

Recognition and measurement of revenue

Introduction

33. 65 Under IFRIC 12, the operator is regarded as a service provider. It provides construction or upgrade services during the construction phase and operational

续表

参考段落	付款结构	经营方所确认基础设施资产的性质	
		金融资产	无形资产
第 33.58 段	使用者基于使用情况向经营方支付款项，而经营方承担需求风险。		√
第 33.58 段	授予方基于使用情况向经营方支付款项，而经营方承担需求风险。		√
第 33.59 段	使用者向经营方付款，但所收费用由监管者调整，以确保经营方获得实质上固定的回报。经营方承担需求风险，即使该风险很低。		√
第 33.59 段	使用者向经营方付款，而特许权持续到经营方达成其投资回报为止。经营方承担特许权期间的需求风险。		√
第 33.62 段	使用者基于使用情况向经营方付款，但授予方担保付款不会低于某一规定最低额（差额担保）。需求风险由授予方和经营方共担。	√（授予方应付最低额）	√（超出使用者应付最低额）

值得注意的是，对金融资产或无形资产的任何确认意味着经营方已向授予方提供了建造或改良服务。如果协议没有涉及任何建造或改良服务，那么就没有资产产生，也没有向授予方或第三方付款的义务（参见下述第 33.102 段）。

收入的确认和计量

引言

33.65　在 IFRIC 12 中，经营方被认为是服务提供者。它在建造阶段期间提供建造或改良服务，并在运营阶段期间提供运营服务。经营方所确认的收入反

services during the operational phase. The revenue recognised by the operator reflects its 'right to receive consideration in exchange for its performance', rather than the cash actually received. The accounting requirements for revenue and profit recognition on construction and service contracts are addressed in IAS 11 and IAS 18. These standards are considered in detail in chapter 9.

Recognition and measurement of construction or upgrade revenue

33.66 The operator should recognise revenue and costs during the construction phase in accordance with IAS 11. [IFRIC 12 para 14]. It requires the revenue to be recognised by reference to the stage of completion of the contract activity. For example, if the concession arrangement's terms require an operator to build a hospital that takes three years to complete, the operator will recognise costs and revenue as the contract activity progresses over the three year period. IAS 11 notes that the stage of completion may be determined in a variety of ways and that the entity should use the method that measures reliably the work performed. [IAS 11 para 30].

33.67 IAS 11 requires revenue from construction or upgrade services to be measured at the fair value of the consideration received or receivable. In most service concession arrangements, the operator is not normally remunerated separately for the construction services provided. Rather, the grantor typically negotiates a single contract with the operator that specifies the total consideration receivable for all the services provided under the contract throughout the concession term. In such cases, the operator will need to allocate the total consideration receivable during the concession period between the construction and operation services.

33.68 Therefore, where the operator provides more than one service (for example, construction services, upgrade services and operations services) under a single contract or arrangement, IFRIC 12 requires the total consideration received or receivable be allocated by reference to the '*relative fair values of the services delivered, when the amounts are separately identifiable*'. [IFRIC 12 para 13].

映其“以其业绩取得对价的权利”，而不是实际的现金所得。对于建造和服务合同收入和利润确认的会计处理要求，在 IAS 11 和 IAS 18 中阐述。上述准则详见第九章。

建造或改良收入的确认和计量

33.66 经营方必须依据 IAS 11，确认建造阶段期间的收入和成本。[IFRIC 12 第 14 段]。该准则要求参照合同活动完成阶段确认收入。例如，如果特许权安排的条款要求经营方建造一家医院，工期为三年，经营方会按照三年期间合同业务的进展确认成本和收入。IAS 11 指出，可以通过多种方式确认完成阶段，而主体必须采用可靠的方法，计量已开展的工作。[IAS 11 第 30 段]。

33.67 IAS 11 要求来自建造或改良服务的收入以已收或应收对价的公允价值计量。在大多数特许服务权安排中，经营方通常不是为其所提供的建造服务被单独支付报酬。而是，授予方通常与经营方商定一份单一合同，在合同中规定特许权期间所提供全部服务的应收对价。在此情况下，经营方将需要在建造和运营服务之间分配特许权期间总的应收对价。

33.68 因此，当经营方根据单一合同或协议，提供一种以上服务（例如，建造服务、改良服务以及运营服务）的情况下，IFRIC 12 要求总的已收对价或应收对价应该参照“*在金额可单独辨认的情况下，所交付服务的相对公允价值*”进行分配。[IFRIC 12 第 13 段]。这与 IAS 18 相一致，IAS 18 要求其确认标准被分别应用于单笔交易的可辨认组成部分，以便反映交易的实质。

This is consistent with IAS 18, which requires its recognition criteria to be applied separately to identifiable components of a single transaction in order to reflect the transaction's substance. [IAS 18 para 13]. The amounts for each service (that is, construction or upgrade service, and operation service) should be identifiable because each separate phase has its own distinct skills, requirements and risks.

33.69 In some service concession arrangements, it may be possible to determine clearly how the total consideration is made up. For example, it may be possible to identify the underlying revenue streams that relate to the different activities because different parts of the contract have been negotiated separately or the contract allows price adjustments for separate elements of the contract by 'market testing' or 'benchmarking'. Such market testing could be done by the grantor or the operator. For instance, if the grantor market tests what it pays for an element of an individual service, with an adjustment made to that payment, then there will be a separately identifiable payment stream. In those circumstances, the fair values of the individual services can be arrived at by discounting the underlying future cash receipts.

33.70 Where it is not possible to separate any of the contract's components because of an inability to reliably determine what the revenue on each of the elements should be, a considerable amount of judgment may be required in measuring the fair value of the consideration received or receivable for the construction services. IAS 18 does not provide further guidance on this point. IFRIC 12 states that, in practice, the fair value of the construction services delivered may be the most appropriate method of establishing the fair value of the consideration received or receivable for the construction services. This will often be the case in service concession arrangements where the consideration attributable to the construction activity often has to be apportioned from a total sum receivable on the contract as a whole and, if it consists of an intangible asset, may also be subject to uncertainty in measurement. [IFRIC 12 para BC30].

33.71 The IFRIC further notes that if the revenue attributable to different activities is allocated by reference to its fair values, the entity might report different profit margins on these different activities. [IFRIC 12 para BC31]. This appears to suggest that where different components of a concession arrangement have

［IAS 18 第 13 段］。每一种服务（即建造或改良，以及运营服务）的金额必须是可辨认的，因为每个单独的阶段有其自身独特的技能、要求和风险。

33.69　在某些特许服务权安排中，也许有可能很清楚地确定总对价的构成方式。例如，也许有可能辨认与不同业务相关的标的收入来源，因为合同的不同部分已经被单独商定，或者合同允许按“市场测试法”或“基准法”对合同独立的组成部分进行价格调整。这种“市场测试”可由授予方或由经营方来执行。例如，如果授予方对单项服务组成部分付款进行市场测试，并对该款项进行调整，那么就有一个单独可辨认的付款来源。在那些情况下，单项服务的公允价值可通过折现未来标的现金收入得出。

33.70　在由于不能可靠地确定每个部分的收入数额，而不能对合同任何组成部分进行分割的情况下，也许需要大量的判断，来计量因建造服务已收或应收对价之公允价值。IAS 18 并未对这一点提供进一步的指引。IFRIC 12 指出，在实务中，所交付建造服务的公允价值可能是确立建造服务的所得或应得对价之公允价值最合适的方法。这在可归于建造业务的对价通常必须从合同应收款总额中进行分配的特许服务权安排中很常见，而且如果含有无形资产，还可能受限于计量不确定性。［IFRIC 12 BC 第 30 段］。

33.71　国际财务报告解释委员会进一步指出，如果可归于不同活动的收入参照其公允价值分配，主体可以按这些不同的活动报告不同的利润率。［IFRIC 12 BC 第 31 段］。这似乎表明，在一个特许服务权安排的不同组成部分具有相当不同的毛利时（特别是建造组成部分和服务组成部分），必须以反映这些

substantially different margins (particularly construction components and service components) , they should be accounted for in a manner that reflects those components. Although a considerable amount of judgement would be required to determine a fair profit margin for different activities, estimates of cost of different activities loaded with an appropriate profit margin may be a reasonable method of allocating the total consideration. The following example, based on the figures used in illustrative example 1 in IFRIC 12, explains how the total purchase consideration can be allocated among the various activities undertaken in a service concession arrangement.

Example – Allocation of consideration between construction and operational services

The arrangement's terms require an operator to construct a road-completing construction within two years-and maintain and operate the road to a specified standard for eight years (that is, years 3 – 10). The terms of the arrangement also require the operator to resurface the road at the end of year 8 – the resurfacing activity is revenue-generating. At the end of year 10, the arrangement will end.

The arrangement's terms require the grantor to pay the operator C200,000 per year in years 3 – 10 for making the road available to the public. For the purpose of this example, it is assumed that all cash flows take place at the end of the year.

The operator estimates that the costs it will incur to fulfil its obligations and the margins that it expects to earn on the various activities will be as follows:

	Year	**Cost**	**Mark up on cost**	**Fair value**
		C'000		**C'000**
Construction services	1	500	5%	525
	2	500	5%	525
Operation services per year	3 – 10	10	20%	12
Major maintenance – road resurfacing	8	100	10%	110

组成部分的方式对它们进行会计处理。尽管需要大量的判断来确定不同业务活动的公允毛利，估算不同活动的成本及恰当的毛利或许是分配总对价的合理方法。下述示例，基于 IFRIC 12 解说性示例 1 中所使用的数据，说明如何在一项特许服务权安排所开展的不同活动间分配总采购对价。

示例——在建造和运营服务间分配对价

协议条款要求经营方在两年内完成建造一条公路，并按规定的标准维护和运营公路8 年（即第 3 年到第 10 年）。此外，协议条款要求经营方在第 8 年年末重新铺设路面——重铺活动是产生收入的。协议将于第 10 年年末结束。

协议条款要求授予方在第3 年到第10 年每年向经营方支付20 万元，以便道路可供公众使用。就本示例而言，假定所有的现金流量都发生在年末。

经营方估算的为履行其义务而将要发生的成本，以及其预期于各种业务所能赚得的毛利如下：

	年	成本	毛利	公允价值
		千元		千元
建造服务	1	500	5%	525
	2	500	5%	525
每年运营服务	3—10	10	20%	12
主要维护——重铺路面	8	100	10%	110

Given that the operator has an unconditional contractual obligation to receive C200,000 per annum during the operation phase and this annual amount must be sufficient to enable the operator to recover all its costs under the contract plus earn a return, it is necessary to allocate the fair value of the consideration between the various services by reference to their relative fair values as explained in paragraph 33.67 above. This is shown in the profile for the entire concession period below. For instance, in year 8, the cash received of C200,000 is allocated to the fair value of the operation services of C12,000, the fair value of the major overhaul of C110,000 and the balance of the consideration of C78,000 is allocated to the receivable for the construction services and will also include an element of finance cost.

Total	1	2	3	4	5	6	7	8	9	10
Fair value of consideration received from grantor		200	200	200	200	200	200	200	200	1,600
Fair value of operation services provided by the operator		(12)	(12)	(12)	(12)	(12)	(122)	(12)	(12)	(206)
Balance attributable to construction services + finance income		188	188	188	188	188	78	188	188	1,394

The total amount of cash received of C1,394,000 over the 8 year period is not representative of the fair value of the construction services provided in years 1 and 2 as it includes some element of contribution towards finance income as a result of the delayed payment pattern. Consequently, as explained in paragraph 33.70 above, in practice, the fair value of the consideration for services delivered would be the most appropriate method of establishing the fair value of the consideration received or receivable for the construction services. As the fair value of the construction services delivered in years 1 and 2 amounts to C1,050,000 in total, the difference between this amount and the consideration receivable of C1,394,000 that is, C344,000 represents finance income.

由于经营方在运营阶段期间拥有每年无条件获得 20 万元的合同义务，而这一年度金额必须足以使经营方收回其合同下的所有成本，外加获得回报，有必要通过参照上述第 33.67 段所解释的相对公允价值，在各种服务之间分配对价的公允价值。其展现在下面整个特许权期间概要之中。例如，于第 8 年，所得之 20 万元现金，分配 12,000 元给运营服务公允价值，11 万元给大修的公允价值，而 78,000 元对价余额分配给建造服务应收款，融资成本部分也将包括在内。

合计	1	2	3	4	5	6	7	8	9	10
来自授予方所得对价的公允价值		200	200	200	200	200	200	200	200	1,600
经营方提供的运营服务的公允价值		(12)	(12)	(12)	(12)	(12)	(122)	(12)	(12)	(206)
可归于建造服务 + 融资收益的余额		188	188	188	188	188	78	188	188	1,394

8 年间的所收的 1,394,000 元现金收入总额并不代表第 1 年和第 2 年所提供建造服务的公允价值，因为其包括了由于延迟付款模式而导致的融资收益贡献的一些组成部分。因而，如上述第 33.70 段中的解释，在实务中，所交付服务对价的公允价值将是确立建造服务所得或应收对价公允价值最恰当的方法。由于第 1 年和第 2 年所交付建造服务的公允价值总额为 1,050,000 元，而此金额与应收对价 1,394,000 元的差额为 344,000 元，代表融资收益。

Contract revenue

The operator recognises contract revenue and costs during the construction phase in accordance with IAS 11. Therefore, the operator will recognise construction revenue and costs in years 1 and 2 of C525,000 and C500,000 respectively and record a profit of C25,000 in each of those years.

As explained above, the revenue of C525,000 in years 1 and 2 will be received in cash from years 3 to 8. The effective interest rate for this series of cash flows can be calculated using a financial calculator or a spreadsheet and amounts to 6.18%. This interest rate is used to measure the amortised cost of the financial asset in accordance with IAS 39 (see para 33.89 below).

The total residual consideration receivable after deducting the fair value of the consideration attributable to the construction services is then allocated to each of the services provided as part of the operations over the entire contract period where a financial asset has been recognised.

Non-cash consideration received for construction services

33.72 The total consideration received by the operator for the services provided is not always in cash. As discussed in paragraph 33.56 above, in some circumstances, the grantor makes a non-cash payment for the construction services, that is, it gives the operator an intangible asset (a licence to charge users of the public service). The intangible asset given by the grantor to the operator in exchange for construction services is recognised in accordance with the principles applicable to contracts for goods or services. The contract is not recognised to the extent it is executory. Executory contracts are contracts under which neither party has performed any of its obligations or both parties have partially performed their obligations to an equal extent. [IAS 37 para 3]. As most service concession arrangements are generally executory when the contract is signed, the operator's asset (representing its accumulating rights to be paid for providing construction services) is recognised as an intangible asset as it performs construction or upgrade services and not on completion of the construction.

合同收入

经营方根据 IAS 11 确认建造阶段期间建造收入和成本。因此，经营方将分别确认第 1 年和第 2 年的建造收入和成本 525, 000 元和 500, 000 元，并记录上述每年利润为 25, 000 元。

如上解释，将在第 3 年至第 8 年分别收到第 1 年和第 2 年的收入 525, 000 元。这一系列现金流量的实际利率可用财务计算器或电子数据表计算，数值为 6. 18%。根据 IAS 39，这一利率被用来计量金融资产的摊余成本（参见下述第 33. 89 段）。

在扣除可归于建造服务对价的公允价值之后总的应收对价的余值，再分配至金融资产确认的整个合同期间每项运营组成部分的所提供的服务。

因建造服务所得的非现金对价

33. 72　经营方因所提供的服务而获得的总对价并不总是现金。如上述第 33. 56 段中的探讨，在某些情况下，授予方为建造服务支付非现金付款，也就是，由授予方给予经营方无形资产（向公共服务使用者收费的许可）。由授予方给予经营方、用以交换建造服务的无形资产，根据适用于货物或服务合同的原则进行确认。在合同待执行的情况不进行确认。待执行合同是指双方均未履行任何义务或双方均同等程度地履行了部分义务的合同。［IAS 37 第 3 段］。由于大多数特许服务权安排在合同签订时一般处于待执行状态，经营方的资产（代表其因提供建造服务而累计的收款权利）在执行建造或改良服务的同时被确认为无形资产，而不是在建造完成时。

33.73 Furthermore, under IAS 18, when goods are delivered or services are rendered (construction services) in exchange for dissimilar goods or services (the licence), the exchange is regarded as a transaction that generates revenue. IAS 18 states that the revenue should be measured at the fair value of the goods or services received, unless that fair value cannot be measured reliably, in which case revenue should be measured at the fair value of goods or services given up, adjusted by the amount of any cash or cash equivalent transferred. [IAS 18 para 12]. Since the fair value of the intangible asset received in a service concession arrangement cannot be measured reliably, the fair value of the construction services provided is used as a proxy for measuring both revenue and the intangible asset. Where an intangible asset is recognised, the entire amount of cash flows received from users during the operational phase is recognised as revenue as well (see below). The argument is that the operator uses the intangible asset recognised during the construction phase to generate revenue from users of the public service as it is consumed.

Example – Intangible asset received for construction services

The terms of a service arrangement require an operator to construct a road—completing construction within two years—and maintain and operate the road to a specified standard for eight years (that is, years 3 - 10). The terms of the arrangement also require the operator to resurface the road when the original surface has deteriorated below a specified condition. The operator estimates that it will have to undertake the resurfacing at the end of year 8. At the end of year 10, the service arrangement will end. The operator estimates that the costs it will incur to fulfil its obligations will be as follows:

	Year	C'000
Construction services (the operator earns a margin of 5% on cost)	1	500
	2	500
Operation services per year	3 – 10	10
Major maintenance – road resurfacing	8	100

The terms of the arrangement allow the operator to collect tolls from drivers using the road. The operator forecasts that vehicle numbers will remain

33.73　此外，根据 IAS 18 的规定，在交付货物或提供服务（建造服务），用以交换不同货物或服务（许可）的情况下，交换被认为是产生收入的交易。IAS 18 认为，收入必须以所收到货物或服务的公允价值计量，除非公允价值无法被可靠计量，在这种情况下，收入必须以所让渡的货物或服务的公允价值计量，并按转让的任何现金或现金等价物的金额进行调整。[IAS 18 第 12 段]。由于在特许服务权安排中所得的无形资产的公允价值无法可靠计量时，所提供建造服务的公允价值被用来作为代替价值，既用来计量收入，又用于计量无形资产。在无形资产被确认的情况下，在运营阶段从使用者处获得的现金流量的全部金额也被确认为收入（参见下文）。其理由是，经营方使用建造阶段确认的无形资产，在公共服务使用者消费时产生收入。

示例——因建造服务所得的无形资产

服务协议的条款要求运营方修建一条公路——在两年内完工——并按规定的标准维护和运营公路 8 年（即第 3 年到第 10 年）。协议条款同时也要求经营方在原来的路面已破损到低于特定状况时重铺路面。经营方预计在第 8 年年末将进行铺设。在第 10 年年末，服务协议结束。经营方预计其履行义务将要发生的成本如下：

	年	千元
建造服务（经营方按成本赚取 5% 的毛利）	1	500
	2	500
每年运营服务	3—10	10
主要维护——重铺路面	8	100

协议条款允许经营方向使用道路的司机收取通行费。经营方预计合同期内车辆数量相同，且在第 3 年至第 10 年每年将收取 20 万元的通行费。

constant over the duration of the contract and that it will receive tolls of C200, 000 in each of years 3 - 10.

For the purpose of this example, it is assumed that all cash flows take place at the end of the year.

Intangible asset

The operator provides construction services to the grantor in exchange for an intangible asset, that is, a right to collect tolls from road users in years 3 - 10. The operator recognises revenue and cost in accordance with IAS 11 by reference to the construction's stage of completion. As discussed above, the operator measures contract revenue at the fair value of the consideration receivable. Thus in each of years 1 and 2 it recognises in its income statement construction revenue of C525, 000, construction cost of C500, 000 and construction profit of C25,000.

During the arrangement's construction phase, the operator's asset (representing its accumulating right to be paid for providing construction services) is classified as an intangible asset (licence to charge users of the infrastructure). The operator capitalises the borrowing costs, estimated at 6.7%, during the arrangement's construction phase as required by IAS 23.

	C'000
Construction services in year 1 at fair value	525
Borrowing cost - C500,000 @ 6.7%	34
Construction services in year 2 at fair value	525
Intangible asset at end of year 2	1,084

Toll revenue

The road users pay for the public services at the same time as they receive them, that is, when they use the road. The operator therefore recognises toll revenue of C200,000 in each of years 3 to 8 as it collects the tolls.

就本示例而言，假设所有现金流量在年末发生。

无形资产

经营方向授予方提供建造服务，用以交换无形资产，也就是，在第 3 年到第 10 年从道路使用者收取通行费的权利。经营方根据 IAS 11，参考建造的完工进度，确认收入和成本。如上述所讨论，经营方以应得对价的公允价值计量合同收入。因此，在第 1 年和第 2 年的每一年，经营方在其利润表中确认 525, 000 元的建造收入、500, 000 元的建造成本和 25, 000 元的建造利润。

在协议的建造阶段期间，经营方的资产（代表其因提供建造服务而被支付的累计权利）被分类为无形资产（向基础设施使用者收费的许可）。经营方依据 IAS 23 的要求，资本化协议建造阶段期间的借款费用，估计为 6. 7%。

	千元
第 1 年建设服务的公允价值	525
借款成本——50 万元 ×6. 7%	34
第 2 年建设服务的公允价值	525
第 2 年年末无形资产	1, 084

通行费收入

道路使用者在获取公共服务，即其使用道路的同时为公共服务付费。因此，经营方在收取通行费的第 3 至第 8 年的中，每年确认 200, 000 元的通行费收入。

Revenue under the financial asset and intangible asset models

33.74 Where an operator provides construction or upgrade services, it recognises revenue as those services are performed in accordance with IAS 11, as discussed above. The operator records the corresponding debtor either as a financial asset (a receivable) where it has a contractual obligation to receive cash or an intangible asset where it has a licence to operate with no contractual obligation to receive cash. One consequence of this requirement is that total cash does not equate total revenue as illustrated in the example below.

Example – Revenue under the financial asset and intangible asset model

An operator builds a road at a cost of C100. The construction profit is C10 and the total cash inflows over the life of the concession are C200.

Under the financial asset model, the operator would recognise construction revenue at its fair value of C110 (cost + profit margin) and a financial asset (receivable) of C110. Of the future cash inflows of C200, C110 would be treated as repaying the receivable, with the remaining C90 being recognised as revenue over the life of the concession. Total revenue would be C200.

In contrast, under the intangible asset model, the operator would recognise the same construction revenue of C110, construction profit of C10 and an intangible asset of C110. Over the concession's life, the intangible asset would be amortised against revenues (which in this case would be from users) of C200. The net position is the same as the financial asset case, but total revenues would be C310 rather than C200.

[IFRIC update September 2004].

33.75 This aspect of IFRIC 12, where total revenue does not equal total cash flow, has not been without controversy. Many of the respondents to the draft interpretation criticised the double recognition of revenue and believed that the result had a negative impact on the usefulness of financial statements. The reason for this rather odd result is that when an operator receives an intangible asset in

在金融资产和无形资产模型之下的收入

33.74　在经营方提供建造或改良服务的情况下，如上所述，在提供服务时根据 IAS 11 确认收入。在经营方拥有获得现金的合同权利的情况下在相应的借方记入金融资产（应收款项），或者在其有运营许可而无获得现金的合同权利的情况下记入无形资产。这一要求的结果是，如下例所示，总现金不等于总收入。

示例——金融资产和无形资产模型下的收入

经营方以 100 元的成本建造一条公路。建造利润为 10 元，而在整个特许权期间内总的现金流入为 200 元。

在金融资产模型下，经营方会以公允价值 110 元（成本 + 毛利）确认建造收入和 110 元的金融资产（应收款项）。在 200 元的未来现金流入中，110 元会被作为偿还应收款项，而余下的 90 元在整个特许权期间内被确认为收入。总收入会是 200 元。

相反，在无形资产模型下，经营方会同样地确认 110 元的建造收入、10 元的建造利润以及 110 元的无形资产。在整个特许权期间内，无形资产会被摊销冲抵 200 元的收入（在此情况下来自使用者）。净头寸与金融资产模型中相同，但总收入会是 310 元，而不是 200 元。

[IFRIC 2004 年 9 月更新]。

33.75　IFRIC 12 的这个方面，在总收入不等于总现金流量的情况下，并非没有争议。许多对解释草案的应答者批评收入的重复确认，并认为其结果对于财务报告的有用性具有负面的影响。这一奇怪的结果的原因在于当经营方以其建造服务交换无形资产时，存在两组而非一组流入和流出。在第一组，在以建造服务交换为无形资产的易货交易中，根据 IAS 18 第 12 段的规定，该

exchange for its construction services, there are two sets of inflows and outflows rather than one. In the first set, the construction services are exchanged for the intangible asset in a barter transaction that generates revenue in accordance with paragraph 12 of IAS 18. In the second set, the operator then uses the intangible asset received from the grantor to generate further revenue from users of the public service. IFRIC 12 notes that this result is not unique to service arrangements within the scope of the interpretation. Any situation in which an entity provides goods or services in exchange for dissimilar asset that is subsequently used to generate revenue would lead to a similar result. [IFRIC 12 BC34].

Recognition and measurement of operations revenue

33.76 The operator should account for revenue and costs relating to operation services in accordance with IAS 18. [IFRIC 12 para 20]. Revenue for the operation services will be recognised when those services are delivered.

Example 1 – Recognition of revenue from users as services are delivered

The terms of a public-to-private service concession arrangement require a private sector operator to finance, build, maintain and operate a car park in a regional town for 20 years. The operator receives parking fees from users based on usage.

In this situation, the operator recognises an intangible asset for the construction services. During the operating phase, the operator will recognise parking fees as revenue when those fees are earned. If users of the car park pay the operator in advance, for example enter into a contract to use the car park for six months, the operator will recognise an obligation in advance of performance and apply the recognition and measurement principles of IAS 18 in order to determine an appropriate basis for recognising revenue.

Example 2 – Recognition of revenue from grantor as services are delivered

A service concession arrangement's terms require a private sector operator to finance, build, maintain and operate a prison for 20 years. The grantor pays the operator an annual sum of £20m per year that increases in line with

易货交易产生收入。在第二组中，经营方使用从授予方收到的无形资产而从公共服务使用者获取现金流入。IFRIC 12 指出，这一结果并不仅局限于本解释公告范围内的服务协议。主体提供商品或劳务以交换在其后被用来产生未来现金收入的不同的资产的任何情况均会导致相似结果。[IFRIC 12 BC 第34段]。

经营收入的确认和计量

33.76　经营方必须根据 IAS 18 对与运营服务有关的收入和成本进行核算。[IFRIC 12 第20段]。运营服务收入会在劳务交付时确认。

示例1——劳务交付时确认来自使用者的收入

公共－私营特许服务权安排的条款要求私营部门经营方在地方城镇融资、建造一个停车场，并维护和运营20年。经营方基于使用情况，从使用者处收取停车费。

在此情况下，经营方针对建造服务确认无形资产。在运营阶段期间，经营方会在赚取停车费的情况下，将停车费确认为收入。如果停车场的使用者预付停车费给经营方，例如签订为期六个月的停车场使用合同，经营方会在执行前确认义务，并采用 IAS 18 的确认和计量原则，确定收入确认的适用基础。

示例2——劳务交付时确认来自授予方的收入

特许服务权安排的条款要求私营部门的经营方融资、建造一座监狱，并维护和运营20年。授予方每年付给经营方一笔2千万英镑的费用，随通货膨胀增加。

inflation.

In this situation, the operator recognises a financial asset for the construction services. During the operating phase, the operator allocates a proportion of the cash receipts that settle the financial asset recognised during the construction phase. The balance is consideration for providing maintenance and operation services that is recognised as revenue is earned as well as finance income.

Allocation of contract revenue during the operation phase

33. 77 Where the operator has an unconditional right to receive cash flows from the grantor, the operator recognises a financial asset. The operator may also be required to provide additional maintenance and operational services as noted in example 2 in paragraph 33. 76 above. To the extent that such services are not the result of the use of an asset under licence the operator will recognise revenue from such services as it is earned and measure revenue at the fair value of the consideration received or receivable. An obligation would be recognised when consideration is received in advance of performance. The operator may be required to provide other services that are revenue generating in nature, in addition to maintenance services. For example, under a service concession arrangement, the operator builds and maintains a hospital. In addition, the operator is remunerated for providing other ancillary services such as cleaning, laundry, catering and security services.

33. 78 Where several services are provided in a single service concession arrangement, the principle discussed in paragraph 33. 68 above applies, that is, the operator is required to allocate the total consideration received or receivable to the various services provided by 'reference to the relative fair value of the services delivered, when the amounts are separately identifiable'. For example, all of the services undertaken in the hospital contract referred to above are identifiable because each element has its own skills, requirements and risks.

33. 79 In practice, determining the fair value of each component may be problematic and judgement may be required. In some circumstances, the grantor

在此情况下，经营方针对建造服务确认金融资产。运营阶段期间，经营方分配一定比例的现金收入，结算建造阶段期间所确认的金融资产。余额作为提供维护和运营服务的对价，被确认为所赚取的收入以及融资收益。

在运营阶段期间合同收入的分配

33.77　在经营方拥有从授予方处无条件获得现金流量权利的情况下，经营方确认金融资产。经营方也可能被要求提供如上述第 33.76 段示例 2 中所述额外的维护和运营服务。在这些服务并非在许可资产使用结果的情况下，经营方会确认这些服务所赚取的收入，并以已收或应收对价的公允价值计量收入。在执行之前获得对价的情况下，须确认义务。除了维护服务外，经营方可能被要求提供其他性质上产生收入的服务。例如，在特许服务权安排之下，经营方建造并维护一座医院。另外，经营方因提供诸如清洁、洗衣、餐饮以及安保等其他辅助性服务而被支付报酬。

33.78　在一个单个的特许服务权安排提供多项服务的情况下，上述第 33.68 段所讨论的原则是适用的，也就是，经营方需要在“当金额可单独辨认时，参照交付服务的相对公允价值”的情况下，在多项服务间分配已收或应收的总对价。例如，上述医院合同中所从事的全部服务均可辨认，因为每项服务都有其技术、要求和风险。

33.79　在实务中，确定每个组成部分的公允价值也许有难度，并可能需要进行判断。在某些情况下，如果单独提供上述服务，授予方可能针对医院所开

may specify a fixed amount per month adjusted for inflation for say, undertaking each of the ancillary services in the hospital contract by reference to what the market would charge for these services, if they were provided independently. In those circumstances, the specified amount will be equivalent to fair value. In other situations, the operator may have to estimate a fair margin for the services offered to determine fair value of each component.

33.80 Given that most service concession arrangements are negotiated as a single contract with a single payment structure throughout the concession period, the fair value of the total consideration that falls to be allocated among the various services provided would need to be determined. This determination will usually be done by discounting the contractual cash flows using an imputed rate of interest as specified in IAS 18. IAS 18 defines the imputed rate of interest as the more clearly determinable of either:

- the prevailing rate for a similar instrument of an issuer with a similar credit rating; or
- a rate of interest that discounts the instrument's nominal amount to the current cash sales price of the goods or services.

[IAS 18 para 11].

33.81 This means that the cash flows can be discounted using a prevailing rate of lending to the grantor and the resulting fair value of the consideration allocated to the estimated fair values of the services rendered. Alternatively, an implicit rate could be obtained by discounting the cash flows to the amount equal to the total fair value of the services rendered (see further para 33.83 below). The difference between the fair value of the consideration receivable and the nominal amount of the consideration is recognised as interest revenue using the effective interest method as set out in IAS 39 [IAS 39 paras 9, AG5 – AG8].

展的每项辅助服务，规定每月固定金额，并作通货膨胀的调整。在这些情况下，所规定的金额将等于公允价值。在其他情况下，经营方可能需要估计所提供服务的公允毛利，以确定每个组成部分的公允价值。

33.80　由于大多数特许服务权安排是以一个单一合同，且在特许权期间采用单一付款结构，将需要确定在所提供各项服务间分配的总对价的公允价值。通常根据 IAS 18 的规定，采用估算利率，通过合同现金流量折现进行确定。IAS 18 将估算利率确定为如下二者更清晰者：

- 具有类似信用等级的发行者发行的类似工具的现时利率；或者

- 用于将工具的名义金额折现为商品或劳务现销价格的利率。

[IAS 18 第 11 段]。

33.81　这意味着可使用授予方贷款现行利率对现金流量进行折现，并将计算所得的对价的公允价值分配至所提供各项服务的估计公允价值。或者，可通过将现金流量折现等于所提供服务公允价值总额获得内含利率（参见下述第 33.83 段）。根据 IAS 39 的规定，应收对价的公允价值和对价的名义金额之间的差额，采用实际利率法，确认为利息收益。[IAS 39 第 9 段、AG 第 5 段—第 8 段]。

Accounting for construction asset

Financial asset

Initial recognition

33.82 As explained in paragraph 33.66 above, during the construction phase revenue (including a margin) is recognised as construction activity progresses under IAS 11. A financial asset is set up; this is recorded under IAS 39 at fair value. The IASB published IFRS 9, in November 2009, which amends paragraphs 23, 24 and 25 of IFRIC 12. This amendment introduces changes to the classification of financial assets (see para 33.84 below). The new standard is effective for annual periods beginning on or after 1 January 2013, but will not change the principles relating to the initial recognition of financial assets recognised under IFRIC 12. Hence, the financial asset is built up from day one and continues to build up until construction activity ceases. The asset is amortised as the operator provides public service and receives cash from the grantor during the operation phase. IFRIC 12 requires the financial asset to be accounted for and disclosed in accordance with the financial instruments standards IAS 32, IAS 39 (or IFRS 9) and IFRS 7. [IFRIC 12 para 23].

33.83 Under IAS 39 or IFRS 9 (once effective), the financial asset is recognised initially at its fair value. The fair value of a long-term loan or receivable is estimated as the present value of all the future cash receipts discounted using the prevailing market rate of interest for a similar instrument (similar as to currency, term, type of interest and other factors) with a similar credit rating. [IAS 39 para AG 64]. Therefore, the receivable in a service concession arrangement would be discounted using the grantor's incremental borrowing rate. However, as IFRIC 12 requires the total consideration received or receivable to be allocated by reference to the relative fair values of the services delivered, this can only be done by determining the rate that at inception of the arrangement causes the aggregate present value of all sums receivable from the grantor to be equal to the fair value of

建造资产的会计处理

金融资产

初始确认

33.82　如上述第33.66段中的解释，根据IAS 11，在建造阶段，收入（包括毛利）随着建造活动进度而确认。金融资产创建；根据IAS 39的规定以公允价值进行记录。国际会计准则理事会于2009年11月发布了IFRS 9，修订了IFRIC 12的第23段、第24段和第25段。这一修订引入金融资产分类的变更（参见下述第33.84段）。新的准则自2013年1月1日或以后开始的年度期间起生效，但不会改变IFRIC 12中金融资产初始确认相关的原则。因此，金融资产从第一天被确认，并持续确认直至建造活动终止。在运营阶段经营方提供公共服务并从授予方处收取现金时，该金融资产进行摊销。IFRIC 12要求根据金融工具准则IAS 32、IAS 39（或IFRS 9）和IFRS 7对金融资产进行核算和披露。[IFRIC 12第23段]。

33.83　根据IAS 39或IFRS 9（一旦生效），金融资产以其公允价值作初始确认。长期贷款或应收款项的公允价值通过使用具有类似信用等级的类似工具（类似的币种、期间、利息类型和其他因素）之现时市场利率对所有未来现金收入折现后的现值作估计。[IAS 39AG第64段]。因此，将使用授予方增量借款利率对特许服务权中的应收款项折现。然而，由于IFRIC 12要求参考交付服务相对公允价值来分配总的已收或应收对价，这只能透过决定在协议开始时使来自授予方的所有应收款项总额的总现值等于协议期间提供的服务的公允价值来决定利率。因此，这一利率类似于IAS 17下内含于租赁的利率。除非是在一个完美的市场里，授予方增量借款利率和实际内含利率不太可能相同。选择合适的利率将会影响利润确认的模式。例如，如果选择授予方的增量借款利率作为折现率，在各项服务组成部分间分配总对价，且这一利率

the services to be provided during the arrangement. This rate is, therefore, similar to the rate implicit in a lease under IAS 17. The grantor's incremental borrowing rate and the effective implicit rate are unlikely to be the same, except in a perfect market. Selection of an appropriate rate will affect the pattern of profit recognition. For instance, if the grantor's incremental borrowing rate is chosen as the discount rate for allocating the total consideration among the various service components and this rate is less than the rate at which the operator can borrow to finance the project, the fair value that is attributable to the operator's services will be higher. This may result in recognising higher profits in the earlier years followed by lower profits or even losses in the later years until the borrowing is repaid. Consequently, the selection of an appropriate rate is important to all service concession arrangements and will depend on the facts and circumstances.

Classification

33.84 Under IFRIC 12, the operator is required to classify the financial asset into one of the following three categories:

- a loan or receivable;
- an available-for-sale financial asset;
- at fair value through profit or loss, if so designated at initial recognition.

[IFRIC 12 para 24].

33.84.1 Once IFRS 9 becomes effective, paragraph 24 of IFRIC 12 is amended so that financial assets are classified either as financial assets at amortised cost or as financial assets measured at fair value through profit or loss. IFRS 9 makes substantive changes to the previous classification rules for financial assets, which are further explained in chapter 12 of IFRS Manual of Accounting – Financial instruments.

33.85 It should be noted that under the current standard, IAS 39, a further 'held-to-maturity' category of financial asset is available. IAS 39 states that a financial asset may not be classified as held-to-maturity if it meets the definition of a loan or receivable. An asset that meets the definition of held-to-maturity will meet the definition of a loan or receivable unless:

低于经营方的项目借款融资利率，则可归属于经营方服务的公允价值就会较高。这可能导致在较早的年份确认较高的利润，紧接着在较晚的年份利润较低，或者甚至出现亏损，直到借款被偿还为止。因此，选择合适的利率对于所有的特许服务权安排非常重要，这取决于事实和环境。

分类

33.84　根据 IFRIC 12，要求经营方将金融资产划分为如下三类之一：

- 贷款或应收款项；
- 可供出售金融资产；
- 如果在初始确认时被指定，以公允价值计量且其变动计入损益。

[IFRIC 12 第 24 段]。

33.84.1　一旦 IFRS 9 生效，那么 IFRIC 12 第 24 段就要修改，使金融资产分类为以摊余成本计量的金融资产或以公允价值计量且其变动计入损益的金融资产。IFRS 9 对之前的金融资产分类规则进行了实质性变动，这在《国际财务报告准则实务指引——金融工具系列》第十二章中作进一步解释。

33.85　值得注意的是，根据现行准则 IAS 39，尚有“持有至到期”的金融资产这一类别。IAS 39 指出，金融资产如果满足贷款或应收款项的定义，就不可分类为持有至到期投资。符合持有至到期投资定义的资产符合贷款或应收款项的定义，除非：

- it is quoted in an active market; or
- the holder may not recover substantially all of its initial investment, other than because of credit deterioration.

33.86 The first condition above is unlikely to apply to financial assets arising on service concession arrangements. Where the second condition applies, the asset must be classified as available-for-sale (if not designated upon initial recognition as at fair value through profit or loss). Consequently, private-to-public service arrangements would not be classified as held-to-maturity investments.

33.87 Under IAS 39 an operator may designate a financial asset at fair value through profit or loss on initial recognition only if it meets one of the three conditions specified in paragraph 9 of IAS 39. The three conditions are not reproduced here (see chapter 6 of IFRS Manual of Accounting – Financial instruments) but, in general, it is unlikely that an operator would classify the infrastructure asset as at fair value through profit or loss in order to reduce or eliminate an accounting mismatch or manage its investment in the service concession asset on a fair value basis. As regards the third condition, the IFRIC noted that potential variations in cash flows arising from the operator's failure to meet performance or efficiency targets would not meet the definition of a derivative as these are non-financial variables that are specific to a party to the contract. [IFRIC 12 para BC12].

33.88 Consequently, until IFRS 9 is effective, the operator typically will have a choice of classification between either loans and receivables or available-for-sale classification. In practice, operators may not wish to classify the financial asset on initial recognition as available-for-sale; first, because of the complexity involved in fair valuing the asset at each balance sheet date (see para 33.89 below) and secondly, because reclassification out of available-for-sale to loans and receivables is not permitted in a subsequent period. As mentioned above, an available-for-sale classification is required where the operator may not recover substantially all of its initial investment, other than as a result of credit deterioration. There might be a situation where, to be entitled to the entire revenue, the operator needs to meet specified quality or efficiency requirements or targets during the concession term. A short fall may arise, for example, where the amounts received from, or at the

■ 其存在一个活跃市场；或者
■ 持有者不能充分收回其全部初始投资，但并非因为信用恶化。

33.86　上述第一个条件不大可能适用于特许服务权安排中产生的金融资产。在适用第二个条件时，资产必须划分为可供出售类（如果未在初始确认时指定为以公允价值计量且其变动计入损益）。因此，公共－私营服务安排不能划分为持有至到期投资。

33.87　根据 IAS 39，只有在符合 IAS 39 第 9 段中规定的三个条件之一时，经营方可以在初始确认时指定金融资产以公允价值计量且变动计入损益。这三个条件不在这里重复（参见《国际财务报告准则实务指引——金融工具系列》第六章），但是，通常情况下，经营方不太可能将基础设施资产分类为以公允价值计量且其变动计入损益，以降低或消除会计不匹配或在公允价值的基础上管理特许服务权资产投资。关于第三个条件，国际财务报告解释委员会指出，经营方未能实现绩效或效率目标而产生的现金流量潜在变化不能满足衍生工具的定义，因为其为特定于合同中某一方的非财务变量。[IFRIC 12 BC 第 12 段]。

33.88　因此，直至 IFRS 9 生效，经营方通常会在贷款和应收款项或可供出售类之间做出选择。在实务中，经营方可能不希望在初始确认时将金融资产划分为可供出售类；首先是因为在每个资产负债表日资产公允价值评估所涉及的复杂性（参见下述第 33.89 段）；其次是在后续期间将资产从可供出售类重分类为贷款和应收款项是不允许的。如上所述，在除了信用恶化所导致的原因外，运营方不能充分收回其全部初始投资时，必须划分为可供出售类。可能出现的情形是，为了赚取全部收入，经营方需要在特许经营安排期间满足特定的质量或效率性的要求或目标。例如在基础设施资产低于特定标准或不可使用的情形下，收入会因从授予方收到或授予方指示下款项的减少而减少。然而，IFRIC 12 的结论基础解释，这种情况本身并不能妨碍金融资产分类为贷款及应收款项。[IFRIC 12 BC 第 44 段]。其原理和在 IAS 11 和 IAS 18 下附业绩条件的商品销售或劳务提供所产生的应收款项的会计处理一般实务是

direction of, the grantor are reduced because the infrastructure asset is below a specified standard or is otherwise unavailable. However, IFRIC 12's basis for conclusions explains that the alone does not prevent a financial asset from being classified as loans and receivables. [IFRIC 12 para BC44]. This rationale is consistent with general practice for accounting for receivables arising from the sale of goods and services with performance conditions under IASs 11 and 18.

33.88.1 IFRS 9 will simplify the accounting in this area as entities applying IFRIC 12 will only have the choice between two categories (see para 33.84.1). However, as described in paragraph 33.87, we consider that it will be unlikely for an entity to classify an asset as at fair value through profit or loss in order to reduce or eliminate an accounting mismatch.

Subsequent measurement

33.89 Subsequent to initial recognition, infrastructure assets recognised as loans and receivables are measured at amortised cost using the effective interest method, while those recognised at fair value through profit or loss and available-for-sale financial asset are measured at fair value. There is a general presumption that fair value can be reliably measured for all financial instruments. Nevertheless, the measurement process can be quite complex and gives rise to numerous issues, particularly for financial assets arising in service concession arrangements for which there is no active market. If there is no active market for a financial instrument, fair value is determined using a valuation technique. Using valuation techniques is by no means an easy task and requires the exercise of a significant amount of judgement. IAS 39 provides guidance on the valuation techniques to be used and these techniques are discussed in chapter 6 of IFRS Manual of Accounting – Financial instruments.

33.90 The effective interest method of amortisation applies whether the financial asset is classified as a loan or receivable or as an available-for-sale financial asset. Interest income calculated using the effective interest method is recognised in the income statement in accordance with IAS 39. [IFRIC 12 para 25]. The effective interest method uses a set of *estimated* future cash flows through the expected life of the financial instruments using all of the financial instrument's contractual terms,

一致的。

33.88.1　IFRS 9 将简化这一领域的会计处理，因为应用 IFRIC 12 的主体只能在两类之间做出选择（参见第 33.84.1 段）。然而，如第 33.87 段所述，我们认为主体不太可能将资产划分为以公允价值计量且其变动计入损益类，以降低或消除会计不匹配。

后续计量

33.89　初始确认之后，确认为贷款和应收款项的基础设施资产按实际利率法以摊余成本计量，而确认为以公允价值计量且其变动计入损益及可供出售金融资产的基础设施资产以公允价值计量。通常假设所有金融资产的公允价值均可可靠计量。然而，计量过程可能很复杂，并产生很多问题，特别是特许服务权安排中产生的金融资产并无活跃市场。如果金融资产无活跃市场，采用估值技术决定公允价值。采用估值技术绝对不是简单易行的任务，要求进行大量的判断。IAS 39 对使用的估值技术提供了指引，且在《国际财务报告准则实务指引——金融工具系列》第六章对这些技术进行了探讨。

33.90　无论金融资产被分类为贷款或应收款项还是或可供出售金融资产，均适用于摊销的实际利率法。根据 IAS 39，使用实际利率法计算的利息收益于利润表确认。[IFRIC 12 第 25 段]。实际利率法使用基于金融工具中金融工具合同条款预期寿命内的预期现金流量，而非合同现金流量。然而，在实务中，实际现金流量鲜与预期相符。在这些情况下，IAS 39 要求对金融资产的账面价值进行调整以反映实际现金，且在环境要求经营方修改其估计现金流量时

rather than *contractual* cash flows. However, in practice, actual cash flows rarely occur in line with expectation. In these circumstances, IAS 39 requires an adjustment to the carrying amount of the financial asset to reflect actual cash and revised estimated cash flows whenever circumstances require the operator to revise its cash flow estimates. The adjustment is recognised as income or expense in the income statement (see chapter 9 of IFRS Manual of Accounting – Financial instruments).

33.91 It should be noted that although an available-for-sale financial asset with fixed or determinable payments should be measured at fair value with changes in fair value recognised directly in other comprehensive income, the amortised cost must still be calculated using the effective interest method to determine interest income. This means that the interest income recognised in profit or loss would be the same irrespective of whether the operator classifies the financial asset as a loan or receivable or as available-for-sale. The amount that would fall to be recognised in other comprehensive income is the difference between fair value and amortised cost at each balance sheet date. Normally, no recycling of any cumulative gain or loss recognised in other comprehensive income will be necessary since at the end of the concession period, the fair value of the financial asset will be the redemption amount, if any. This means that changes in fair value arising during the concession period would have netted down to nil. Where, in the unlikely event, the financial asset is classified on initial recognition as at fair value through profit or loss, all changes in fair value are recognised in the income statement.

33.92 All financial assets, except those classified as at fair value through profit or loss, should be reviewed for impairment at each balance sheet date in accordance with IAS 39. If there is objective evidence of impairment, the operator should measure and record the impairment loss in the reporting period. IAS 39 provides examples of factors that may, either individually or taken together, provide sufficient objective evidence that an impairment loss has been incurred on a financial asset or group of financial assets (see chapter 6 of IFRS Manual of Accounting – Financial instruments).

33.92.1 As explained in paragraph 33.84.1, with the introduction of IFRS 9 the available-for-sale classification of financial assets under IAS 39 is no longer

修改估计的现金流量。调整数在利润表中确认为收益或费用（参见《国际财务报告准则实务指引——金融工具系列》第九章）。

33.91 值得注意的是，尽管具有固定或可确定付款的可供出售金融资产必须以公允价值计量且其变动直接在其他综合收益中确认，必须仍采用实际利率法计算摊余成本以决定利息收益。这意味着无论经营方将金融资产分类为贷款或应收款项或可供出售类，在损益中确认的利息收益均相同。在其他综合收益中确认的金额为每个资产负债表日公允价值和摊余成本间的差额。通常情况下，在其他综合收益中确认的累计利得或损失无需转回，因为在特许权期末金融资产的公允价值如果存在即为赎回金额。这意味着，特许权期间产生的公允价值变动将会减少到零。在可能性较小的情况下，金融资产在初始确认时分类为以公允价值计量且其变动计入损益，其公允价值的所有变动在利润表中确认。

33.92 根据IAS 39，所有金融资产，除以公允价值计量且其变动计入损益，均应在每个资产负债表日进行减值评估。如果存在减值的客观证据，经营方应计量和记录报告期间的减值损失。IAS 39 提供了因素示例，这些因素可能单独或整体为金融资产或一组金融资产发生减值提供充分的客观证据（参见《国际财务报告准则实务指引——金融工具系列》第六章）。

33.92.1 如第33.84.1段中所解释的，随着IFRS 9的引入，IAS 39中的可供出售金融资产分类不再可用。因此，特许服务权安排下的金融资产或以公允

available. Hence financial assets under service concession arrangements are either held at fair value through profit or loss or at amortised cost. For assets held at fair value, the accounting will follow the guidance set out in paragraph 33. 89. For assets held at amortised cost the guidance as set out in paragraph 33. 90 will apply in calculating the amortisation required under the effective interest method. Furthermore, the impairment principles as set out in IAS 39 for assets held at amortised cost will also apply under IFRS 9.

Intangible asset

Initial recognition

33. 93 Consistent with the recognition of a financial asset, where the operator is granted the right to charge users, an intangible asset is set up as the operator recognises revenue, being the fair value of the construction services provided during the construction phase. That is, the intangible asset is built up from day one and continues to build up until the construction activity ceases. The asset is recorded in accordance with IAS 38 at cost, that is at the fair value of the construction services provided. [IFRIC 12 para 26].

Subsequent measurement

33. 94 After initial recognition, the operator may choose to measure the intangible asset at cost or fair value that is determined by reference to an active market. [IAS 38 para 75]. This option is not available to the operator because the licence to charge users will not be traded in an active market. Consequently, the intangible asset will be measured at cost less accumulated amortisation and impairment losses.

Amortisation

33. 95 Service concession arrangements normally have a finite term, although the term may be fairly long. Therefore, the useful life of an intangible asset recognised in a service concession arrangement is the arrangement's term. The intangible asset

价值计量且其变动计入损益，或以摊余成本计量。对以公允价值计量的资产，其会计处理应遵循第 33. 89 段中列出的指引。对以摊余成本计量的资产，第 33. 90 段中列出的指引将适用于实际利率法摊余成本计算。此外，IAS 39 中列出的针对以摊余成本计量的资产的减值原则在 IFRS 9 中也同样适用。

无形资产

初始确认

33. 93　与金融资产的确认相一致，在经营方被授予向公共服务使用者收费的权利时，经营方确认一项无形资产，同时确认收入，金额为建造阶段所提供的建造服务的公允价值。换言之，该无形资产产生于整个建造期间。该项资产根据 IAS 38 以成本记录，成本为提供的建造服务的公允价值。[IFRIC 12 第 26 段]。

后续计量

33. 94　在初始确认后，经营方可选择以成本或者通过参考活跃市场确定的公允价值计量无形资产。[IAS 38 第 75 段]。然而，由于向使用者收费的许可并不会在活跃市场上交易，对于经营方而言，此选择并不存在。因此，该无形资产将会以成本减去累计摊销和减值损失计量。

摊销

33. 95　特许服务权安排通常具有期限，尽管该期限可能较长。因此，特许服务权安排中确认的无形资产的使用寿命是安排的期限。无形资产将在其寿命内进行系统摊销。即使基础设施可能有重大余值，鉴于经营方需要在安排终

will be amortised on a systematic basis over that life. The residual value of a finite life intangible asset should be assumed to be zero because, when the concession comes to an end or the contract is transferred to another party, the operator ceases to charge users and the licence expires, even though the infrastructure may have a significant residual value. Therefore, the depreciable amount will be equal to original cost from the operator's perspective.

33.96 Amortisation should commence when the asset is available for use, that is, at the point in time when the operator exercises its rights under the licence to charge users. This may be a period of time after the construction asset is actually brought into use. For example, in some concession arrangements that give rise to a financial asset as well as an intangible asset, the arrangement's terms may give the operator an unconditional right to receive cash from the grantor during the concession's early years before the operator can charge users for the service. In that situation, it would be appropriate for the operator to delay amortisation until such time as it begins to charge users. However, until then the intangible asset should be reviewed for impairment at each reporting date (see para 33.95 above).

33.97 A variety of amortisation methods is allowed under IAS 38. These methods include the straight-line method, the diminishing balance method and the unit of production method. [IFRIC 12 para BC64]. However, the 'interest' method of amortisation that takes into account the time value of money is not permitted. [IFRIC 12 para BC65]. The method used is selected on the basis of the expected pattern of consumption of the expected future economic benefits embodied in the asset. This does not mean that the intangible asset arising on a service concession arrangement would be amortised in line with the recognition of revenue flows. This is because such a method is unlikely to reflect the pattern in which the economic benefits inherent in the infrastructure asset are consumed. Generally, the straight-line method of amortisation is likely to be the most appropriate.

Impairment

33.98 Impairment of intangible assets is dealt with in IAS 36. The operator should assess at each reporting date whether there is any indication that the

止时或合同转移至其他方时停止向使用者收费，即该许可到期，所以相关有限寿命的无形资产余值应假设为零。因此，从经营方的角度来看，应折旧金额将等于原始成本。

33.96　摊销应在资产可供使用时开始，即在经营方根据许可行使权利向使用者收费开始。这可能在建造资产实际投入使用后的某一期间。例如，在某些产生金融资产及无形资产的许可安排下，该安排条款可能赋予经营方在其能够向服务使用者收费前，在特许权安排的前期无条件从授予方获取现金的权利。在此情况下，对于经营方而言，将摊销推迟至其开始向使用者收费时较为合适。然而，直至开始摊销前，主体应在每个报告日对该无形资产作减值复核（参见上述第33.95段）。

33.97　IAS 38允许采用各类摊销方法。这些方法包括直线法、余额递减法和生产总量法。[IFRIC 12 BC第61段]。然而，准则并不允许使用考虑了货币时间价值的“利息”法。[IFRIC 12 BC第65段]。主体应根据该资产预期未来经济利益的消耗方式来选择其摊销方法。这并不意味着特许服务权安排中产生的无形资产的摊销必须与其收入流相一致。这是因为这一方法不大可能反映该基础设施资产内在经济利益的消耗方式。一般来说，直线摊销法可能最为合适。

减值

33.98　无形资产减值根据IAS 36进行处理。经营方需在每个报告日评估无形资产是否存在减值迹象。如果存在迹象，主体需估算资产的可收回金额。如

intangible asset is impaired. If such an indication exists the entity should estimate the asset's recoverable amount. If the recoverable amount is below the asset's carrying amount, the asset should be written down to its recoverable amount.

33.99 The recoverable amount of an intangible asset is the higher of fair value less cost to sell and its value in use. In a service concession arrangement fair value less cost to sell is unlikely to be relevant; hence the operator will use the intangible's asset value in use as its recoverable amount. Under IAS 36, the recoverable amount should be determined for the smallest cash generating unit to which the intangible asset belongs, if the intangible asset does not generate cash flows that are largely independent of those from other assets. This is unlikely to be relevant because the intangible asset in a service concession arrangement itself generates cash flows directly from the public. The way in which the operator should go about estimating value in use of the arrangement and the various factors that it should consider in determining that value are discussed in chapter 18.

Arrangements that contain both financial and intangible asset

33.100 So far, we have described the recognition and measurement of service concession arrangements where the operator recognises either a financial asset or an intangible asset for the construction services it provides to the grantor. However, as noted in paragraph 33.61 above, in some service concession arrangements, typically transport concessions, both parties to the contract share the risk (demand risk) that cash flows from the arrangement will not be sufficient to cover the operator's investment in the infrastructure asset. In such situations, the grantor normally contributes a certain amount but gives the operator the right to charge users for the services. The operator's infrastructure asset is then split between a guaranteed financial component and an unguaranteed intangible component. The recognition and measurement principles described above for individual arrangements apply equally to such composite arrangements.

33.101 Where an arrangement contains both financial and intangible assets, the accounting can be quite complex. Careful judgement and sound systems are

果可收回金额低于资产的账面价值，该资产需调减至其可收回金额。

33.99 无形资产的可收回金额为公允价值减去处置费用与其使用价值两者之中的孰高者。在特许服务权安排中，公允价值减去处置费用不太可能相关；因此，经营方将使用无形资产的使用价值作为其可收回金额。根据 IAS 36，如果无形资产不能基本上独立于其他资产而产生现金流，应根据无形资产所属的最小现金产出单元确定其可收回金额。因为特许服务权安排中的无形资产自身可直接从公众产生现金流量，所以这也不太可能相关。有关经营方估计安排的使用价值的方式及估算使用价值时需考虑的各项因素的讨论请参见第十八章。

同时包含金融资产和无形资产的安排

33.100 至此，我们已经描述了经营方将其向授予方提供的建造服务确认为金融资产或者无形资产的特许服务权安排的确认和计量。然而，如上述第 33.61 段中提及，在某些特许服务权安排，特别是在运输业的安排中，合同双方会共同承担安排中现金流量不足以回收经营方对基础设施资产投资的风险（需求风险）。在此情况下，授予方通常付出一定金额，但同时给予经营方向服务使用者收费的权利。因此，经营方的基础设施资产被划分为担保金融资产组成部分和未担保无形资产组成部分。上述的单项安排确认和计量原则同等适用于此综合安排。

33.101 在安排中包含金融资产和无形资产的情况下，会计处理可能十分复杂。在特许权期间，谨慎的判断和健全的系统来统计和核算安排里的所有特

necessary to track and account for all the features of the arrangement during the concession period. Illustrative example 3 in the interpretation sets out in detail how an operator should account for such a composite arrangement. The example, modified in some respects, is reproduced below. The example deals with only one of many possible types of arrangements. Its purpose is to illustrate the accounting treatment for some features that are commonly found in practice. To make the illustration as clear as possible, it has been assumed that the arrangement period is only ten years and that the operator's annual receipts are constant over that period. In practice, arrangement periods may be much longer and annual revenues may increase with time. In such circumstances, the changes in net profit from year to year could be greater.

Example – Arrangements containing both financial and intangible assets

The terms of a service arrangement require an operator to construct a road – completing construction within two years – and to operate the road and maintain it to a specified standard for eight years (that is, years 3 – 10). The terms of the arrangement also require the operator to resurface the road when the original surface has deteriorated below a specified condition. The operator estimates that it will have to undertake the resurfacing at the end of year 8. At the end of year 10, the arrangement will end. The operator estimates that the costs it will incur to fulfil its obligations will be as follows:

Table 1 – Contract costs

	Year	C'000
Construction services	1	500
	2	500
Operation services per year	3 – 10	10
Major maintenance – road resurfacing	8	100

The operator estimates the consideration in respect of construction services to be cost plus 5%.

The terms of the arrangement allow the operator to collect tolls from drivers

征是必不可少的。解释公告中的示例 3 详细阐述了经营方应该如何核算此类综合安排。如下为基于该示例但在某些方面经过修改后的例子。本例子仅针对众多安排类型中的一种。目的旨在说明实务中普遍存在的某些特征的会计处理。为了让例子尽量清晰，假定安排期间仅为 10 年，且经营方的年收入于经营期内保持不变。实务中，安排期间可能更长且年收入可能会随着时间逐渐增加。在这种情况下，每年净利润的变动会更大。

示例——包含金融资产和无形资产的安排

服务安排条款要求经营方修建一条公路，在两年内完工，并以特定标准运营和维护公路 8 年（即第 3 年至第 10 年）。安排的条款同时也要求经营方在当原来的路面已破损到低于特定状况时重铺路面。经营方估计在第 8 年末将进行重铺。在第 10 年末，安排将结束。经营方估计其履行义务将发生的成本如下：

图表 1——合同成本

	年	千元
建造服务	1	500
	2	500
每年经营性服务	3—10	10
主要维护工作——重铺路面	8	100

经营方估计建造服务的对价为成本加成 5%。

安排的条款允许经营方向使用公路的司机收取通行费。另外，授予方保

using the road. In addition, the grantor guarantees the operator a minimum amount of C700,000 and interest at a specified rate of 6.18% to reflect the timing of cash receipts. The operator forecasts that vehicle numbers will remain constant over the duration of the contract and that it will receive tolls of C200,000 in each of years 3 – 10.

The operator capitalises the borrowing costs in accordance with IAS 23, estimated at 6.7% during the construction phase.

For the purpose of this example, it is assumed that all cash flows take place at the end of the year.

Dividing the arrangement

The contractual right to receive cash from the grantor for the services and the right to charge users for the services should be regarded as two separate assets under IFRSs. Therefore, in this arrangement it is necessary to divide the operator's consideration, which is measured at the fair value of the consideration services provided, into two components – a financial asset component based on the guaranteed amount and an intangible asset for the remainder.

Table 2 – Dividing the operator's consideration

	Total	**Financial asset**	**Intangible asset**
Year 1 Construction services (C500 × (1 + 5%))	525	350	175
Year 2 Construction services (C500 × (1 + 5%))	525	350	175
Total construction services	1,050	700	350
Finance income at a specified rate of 6.18% on receivable (see table 3)	22	22	—
Borrowing cost capitalised (interest paid in years 1 and 2 × 33% (see table 7)	11	—	11
Total fair value of operator's consideration	1,083	722	361

证经营方至少可以获得700,000元和以6.18%特定利率计算的利息以反映现金流入的时间价值。经营方预测合同期内车辆数量将维持不变，且在第3年至第10年每年将收取200,000元的通行费。

经营方根据IAS 23，将估算的建设期间6.7%的借款费用于建设期间予以资本化。

就本示例而言，假设所有的现金流量都发生在年末。

安排分割

于国际财务报告准则下，因服务而从授予方收取现金的合同权利和因提供公共服务而向使用者收费的权利被认为是两项不同的资产。所以，在这一安排中，有必要把经营方的以相关服务的公允价值确认的对价分为两部分——基于保证金额的金融资产部分和剩余部分作为无形资产。

图表2——对经营方对价的分割

	合计	金融资产	无形资产
第1年的建造服务（500元 ×（1 + 5%））	525	350	175
第2年的建造服务（500元 ×（1 + 5%））	525	350	175
建造服务总额	1,050	700	350
对应收款项按6.18%的特定利率计算的融资收益（见图表3）	22	22	—
借款费用资本化（第1年和第2年支付的利息 × 33%，见图表7）	11	—	11
经营方对价的公允价值总额	1,083	722	361

Financial asset

The Financial asset meets the definition of a loan or receivable under IAS 39. It is initially measured at fair value and subsequently measured at amortised cost. The receivable balance at the end of the construction period is C722 as shown above. It carries interest at a specified rate of 6. 18% each year. The receivable will reduce to zero at the end of year 10. Therefore, the amount of cash receipts in each period (years 3 to 10) that will reduce an opening receivable balance of C722 that carries interest at 6. 18% , calculated using a financial calculator or an excel spreadsheet, amounts to C117 as shown below:

Table 3 – Measurement of receivable

	1	2	3	4	5	6	7	8	9	10
Opening balance		350	722	650	573	491	404	312	214	110
Construction service	350	350								
Interest income @ 6. 18% of opening balance		22	45	40	35	30	25	19	13	7
Cash received			(117)	(117)	(117)	(117)	(117)	(117)	(117)	(117)
Closing balance	350	722	650	573	491	404	312	214	110	nil

Intangible asset

During the construction phase of the arrangement the operator's asset (representing its accumulating right to be paid for providing construction services) is classified as a right to receive a licence to charge users of the infrastructure (an intangible asset). The intangible asset is recorded at the fair value of the consideration received or receivable. The operator estimates the fair value of its consideration received or receivable as equal to the forecast construction costs plus 5% . The operator also capitalises borrowing costs, estimated at 6. 7% , during the construction phase. The intangible asset is amortised on a straight line basis. The carrying value throughout the concession period is shown below:

金融资产

该金融资产符合 IAS 39 中贷款或应收款项的定义。它以公允价值进行初始计量，以摊余成本作为后续计量。如上所示，建造期末的应收款项余额为 722 元。每年的特定利率为 6.18%。在第 10 年年末，应收款项将减少为零。因此，通过每期（第 3 年至第 10 年）收取现金以将附带 6.18% 利息的期初应收款项余额 722 元减少为零的每期应收金额为 117 元，使用财务计算器或电子表格的计算如下：

图表 3——应收账款的计量

	1	2	3	4	5	6	7	8	9	10
期初余额		350	722	650	573	491	404	312	214	110
建造服务	350	350								
融资收益，期初余额的 6.18%		22	45	40	35	30	25	19	13	7
现金收入			(117)	(117)	(117)	(117)	(117)	(117)	(117)	(117)
期末余额	350	722	650	573	491	404	312	214	110	0

无形资产

在安排的建造期间，经营方资产（代表其因提供建造服务而要求支付的累计权利）被划分为向基础设施使用者收取使用费权利的许可（无形资产）。无形资产以其已收或应收对价的公允价值进行记录。经营方估计其已收或应收对价的公允价值等于预计建造成本加 5%。经营方在建造期间也以 6.7% 来资本化借款费用。无形资产采用直线法摊销。安排期间的账面价值如下：

Table 4 – Measurement of intangible asset

	1	2	3	4	5	6	7	8	9	10
Opening balance		175	361	316	271	226	181	136	91	46
Construction service	175	175								
Borrowing costs capitalised		11								
Amortisation			45	45	45	45	45	45	45	46
Closing balance	175	361	316	271	226	181	136	91	46	nil

Contract revenue and costs

Construction phase

The operator provides construction services to the grantor in exchange for a financial asset and an intangible asset. Under both the financial asset model and intangible asset model, the operator recognises contract revenue and costs in accordance with IAS 11, that is, by reference to the stage of completion of the construction. It measures contract revenue at the fair value of the consideration receivable. Thus in each of years 1 and 2 it recognises in its income statement construction costs of C500 and construction revenue of C525 (cost plus 5%).

Operation phase

During the operation phase, the operator receives toll revenue from the public. The road users pay for the public services at the same time as they receive them, that is, when they use the road. The operator allocates the receipts from tolls between repayment of the financial asset and revenue earned from the intangible asset.

图表 4——无形资产的计量

	1	2	3	4	5	6	7	8	9	10
期初余额		175	361	316	271	226	181	136	91	46
建造服务	175	175								
资本化的借款费用		11								
摊销			45	45	45	45	45	45	45	46
期末余额	175	361	316	271	226	181	136	91	46	0

合同收入和成本

建造阶段

经营方向授予方提供建造服务来换取金融资产和无形资产。在金融资产模型和无形资产模型下，经营方根据 IAS 11 来确认合同收入和成本，即根据建造完工程度。经营方以应收对价的公允价值来计量合同收入。所以在第 1 年和第 2 年的每一年，经营方在损益中都将确认 500 元的建造成本和 525 元的建造收入（成本加成 5%）。

运营阶段

在运营期间，经营方从公众获得通行费收入。公路使用者在接受公共服务的同时，即当他们在使用公路时为其付费。经营方把通行费收入在偿付金融资产和无形资产赚取的收入之间进行分配。

Table 5 – Allocation of toll revenue

	1	2	3	4	5	6	7	8	9	10
Toll received from users			200	200	200	200	200	200	200	200
Repayment of financial asset (see table 3)			(117)	(117)	(117)	(117)	(117)	(117)	(117)	(117)
Revenue from intangible asset			83	83	83	83	83	83	83	83

Resurfacing obligations

The operator's resurfacing obligation arises as a consequence of use of the road during the operation phase. It isrecognised and measured in accordance with IAS 37, that is, at the best estimate of the expenditure required to settle the present obligation at the balance sheet date.

For the purpose of this example, it is assumed that the terms of the operator's contractual obligation are such that the best estimate of the expenditure requiredto settle the obligation at any date is proportional to the number of vehicles that have used the road by that date and increases by C17 each year. The operator discounts the provision to its present value in accordance with IAS 37. The discount rate is 5%. The income statement charge each period is:

Table 6 – Resurfacing obligation

	3	4	5	6	7	8
Opening provision		12	26	41	58	78
Charged to the income statement:						
Obligation arising in year (C17 discounted @ 5%)	12	13	14	15	16	17
Increase due to passage of time		1	1	2	4	5
	12	14	15	17	20	22
Utilised in year						(100)
Closing provision	12	26	41	58	78	nil

图表 5——通行费收入的分配

	1	2	3	4	5	6	7	8	9	10
从使用者收取的通行费			200	200	200	200	200	200	200	200
金融资产偿付（见图表 3）			(117)	(117)	(117)	(117)	(117)	(117)	(117)	(117)
来自无形资产的收入			83	83	83	83	83	83	83	83

重铺路面义务

经营方重铺路面义务来自于在运营期间对公路的使用。该义务根据 IAS 37 进行确认和计量，即以资产负债表日的现时义务所需支出的最佳估计来确认和计量。

此示例假设经营方的合同义务用于偿付任何一天的支出的最佳估计为与当天使用公路的汽车数量成比例，并且每年递增 17 元。经营方根据 IAS 37 对预计负债进行折现。折现率为 5%。每期在损益表中确认的费用为：

图表 6——重铺路面义务

	3	4	5	6	7	8
期初预计负债		12	26	41	58	78
计入损益：						
年度义务（17 元按 5% 折现）	12	13	14	15	16	17
时间价值		1	1	2	4	5
	12	14	15	17	20	22
年度使用						(100)
期末预计负债	12	26	41	58	78	0

Overview of cash flows, income statement and balance sheet

For the purposes of this example, it is assumed that the operator finances the arrangement wholly with debt and retained profits. It pays interest at 6.7% per year on outstanding net debt. If the cash flows and fair values remain the same as those forecast, the operator's cash flows, income statement and balance sheet over the duration of the arrangement will be:

Table 7 – Cash flows

	1	2	3	4	5	6	7	8	9	10	Total
Receipts			200	200	200	200	200	200	200	200	1,600
Contract costs	(500)	(500)	(10)	(10)	(10)	(10)	(10)	(110)	(10)	(10)	(1,180)
Borrowing costs on net debt@ 6.7%		(34)	(69)	(61)	(53)	(43)	(33)	(23)	(19)	(7)	(342)
Net inflow/ (outflow)	(500)	(534)	121	129	137	147	157	67	171	183	78
Net debt											
Opening balance		(500)	(1,034)	(913)	(784)	(647)	(500)	(343)	(276)	(105)	–
Net inflow/ (outflow)	(500)	(534)	121	129	137	147	157	67	171	183	78
Closing balance	(500)	(1,034)	(913)	(784)	(647)	(500)	(343)	(276)	(105)	78	78

现金流量、利润表以及资产负债表概览

示例假设经营方全部采用债务和未分配利润为该安排提供融资。对未到期的净债务按年利率6.7%支付利息。如果现金流量和公允价值与预期相同，经营方在安排期间的现金流量、利润表和资产负债表应为：

图表7——现金流量

	1	2	3	4	5	6	7	8	9	10	合计
收入			200	200	200	200	200	200	200	200	1,600
合同成本	(500)	(500)	(10)	(10)	(10)	(10)	(10)	(110)	(10)	(10)	(1,180)
借款费用（净债务的6.7%）		(34)	(69)	(61)	(53)	(43)	(33)	(23)	(19)	(7)	(342)
净流入/（流出）	(500)	(534)	121	129	137	147	157	67	171	183	78
净债务											
期初余额		(500)	(1,034)	(913)	(784)	(647)	(500)	(343)	(276)	(105)	-
净流入/（流出）	(500)	(534)	121	129	137	147	157	67	171	183	78
期末余额	(500)	(1,034)	(913)	(784)	(647)	(500)	(343)	(276)	(105)	78	78

Table 8 – Income statement

	1	2	3	4	5	6	7	8	9	10	Total
Revenue on construction	525	525									1,050
Revenue from intangible asset			83	83	83	83	83	83	83	83	664
Total revenue	525	525	83	83	83	83	83	83	83	83	1,714
Construction costs	500	500									1,000
Operating costs			10	10	10	10	10	10	10	10	80
Resurfacing costs			12	14	15	17	20	22			100
Amortisation			45	45	45	45	45	45	45	46	361
Total operating costs	500	500	67	69	70	72	75	77	55	56	1,541
Operating profit	25	25	16	14	13	11	8	6	28	27	173
Net Finance cost											
Borrowing cost		(23)*	(69)	(61)	(53)	(43)	(33)	(23)	(19)	(7)	(331)
Finance income		22	45	40	35	30	25	19	13	7	236
		(1)	(24)	(21)	(18)	(13)	(8)	(4)	(6)	–	(95)
Net profit/(loss)	25	24	(8)	(7)	(5)	(2)	–	2	22	27	78

* Borrowing costs incurred during the period is C34 of which C11 is capitalised.

Note, the large volatility in profits from year to year. The operator recognises greater profits during the construction phase, followed by losses due to high net borrowing costs and finally profits towards the later stages.

Table 9 – Balance sheet

	1	2	3	4	5	6	7	8	9	10
Intangible asset	175	361	316	271	226	181	136	91	46	nil
Loan or receivable	350	722	650	573	491	404	312	214	110	nil
Net debt	(500)	(1,034)	(913)	(784)	(647)	(500)	(343)	(276)	(105)	78
Resurfacing obligation			(12)	(26)	(41)	(58)	(78)			
Net assets	25	49	41	34	29	27	27	29	51	78

图表 8——利润表

	1	2	3	4	5	6	7	8	9	10	合计
建造收入	525	525									1,050
来自于无形资产的收入			83	83	83	83	83	83	83	83	664
收入合计	525	525	83	83	83	83	83	83	83	83	1,714
建造成本	500	500									1,000
经营成本			10	10	10	10	10	10	10	10	80
重铺路面成本			12	14	15	17	20	22			100
摊销			45	45	45	45	45	45	45	46	361
经营成本合计	500	500	67	69	70	72	75	77	55	56	1,541
经营利润	25	25	16	14	13	11	8	6	28	27	173
净财务成本											
借款成本		(23)*	(69)	(61)	(53)	(43)	(33)	(23)	(19)	(7)	(331)
融资收益		22	45	40	35	30	25	19	13	7	236
		(1)	(24)	(21)	(18)	(13)	(8)	(4)	(6)	–	(95)
净利润/(亏损)	25	24	(8)	(7)	(5)	(2)	–	2	22	27	78

* 当期所产生的借款费用为 34 元,其中资本化了 11 元。

附注:每年利润变化很大。经营方在建造期间确认的利润较高,紧接着由于高额的借款费用净额而发生亏损,最终在后期获取利润。

图表 9——资产负债表

	1	2	3	4	5	6	7	8	9	10
无形资产	175	361	316	271	226	181	136	91	46	–
贷款或应收款项	350	722	650	573	491	404	312	214	110	–
净负债	(500)	(1,034)	(913)	(784)	(647)	(500)	(343)	(276)	(105)	78
重铺路面义务			(12)	(26)	(41)	(58)	(78)			
净资产	25	49	41	34	29	27	27	29	51	78

Cash flow relating to construction services

33. 101. 1 In November 2011, the IFRS IC considered whether all of the cash flows relating to construction services under a service concession arrangement should be presented as operating or investing cash flows. The IFRS IC noted that the principle in IAS 7 is to classify cash flows in a manner that is consistent with the activity that generated them. In the case of construction services in a service concession arrangement, that is an operating activity. Hence it is more appropriate to present the cash flows as operating cash flows.

Other matters

Arrangement does not give rise to construction or upgrade services

33. 102 Service concession arrangements need not necessarily involve the operator undertaking construction or upgrade activities. The grantor can give access to the operator to its existing assets for the purpose of the public service arrangement that requires little or no upgrade. In consideration for providing the public service, the grantor may pay the operator directly, or give the operator the right to charge users based on usage, but pricing is regulated. Although this type of arrangement falls within the scope of paragraph 7 (b) of IFRIC 12 as noted in paragraph 33. 27 above, IFRIC 12 does not specifically deal with situations where the public service arrangement consists only of an operation phase and no construction phase. Consider the following example:

Example – Arrangement does not give rise to construction or upgrade services

A public service organisation currently provides a bus service in a town with a population of 500,000. It decides to hand over the running of the bus service to a private sector operator. The private sector operator is given access to all

建造服务相关的现金流量

33.101　2011 年 11 月，国际财务报告准则解释委员会考虑服务特许权安排中与建造服务相关的所有现金流量是否应列报为经营现金流还是投资现金流。国际财务报告准则解释委员会注意到，IAS 7 中的原则是将现金流量按照与产生现金流的活动相一致的方式分类。在服务特许权安排中的建造服务为经营性活动。因此，将现金流量列报为经营性现金流量更为合适。

其他事项

不存在建造或改良服务的安排

33.102　服务特许权安排并不一定涉及经营方从事建造或改良活动。授予方可以让经营方使用其现有资产，用于公共服务安排的目的，且该资产很少需要或不需要升级。对于提供公共服务的对价，授予方可以直接支付给经营方，或者给予经营方依据使用情况向使用者收费的权利，但定价受到监管。尽管这一类型的安排如上述第 33.27 段提及的属于 IFRIC 12 第 7（b）段的范围，但是 IFRIC 12 并未专门针对涉及只包含运营阶段而不包含建造阶段的公共服务安排进行讨论。考虑如下示例：

示例——不存在建造或改良服务的安排

一个公共服务机构目前在一个 50 万人口的城镇提供巴士服务。它决定将巴士服务运营交给私营部门经营方。私营部门经营方被允许使用所有用于运营和维护服务的基础设施资产（巴士车队、巴士站、车库、维修和

infrastructure assets that are used for operating and maintaining the service (fleet of buses, bus stations, garages, repair and maintenance equipment etc). The concession period is 10 years at the end of which the infrastructure reverts back to the grantor. There is no provision to upgrade or expand the network (introduce new routes etc). The operator has a contractual obligation to maintain the infrastructure to a specified level of serviceability and to restore the infrastructure to a specified condition before it is handed over to the grantor at the end of the service arrangement.

As stated above, this type of arrangement falls within IFRIC 12's scope and, consequently, the arrangement is scoped out of IFRIC 4.

The way in which an operator would account for such an arrangement in the absence of any specific guidance in IFRIC 12 is illustrated below:

Scenario 1 – Grantor pays the operator a fixed sum

In this situation, the grantor pays the operator a fixed sum per annum throughout the 10 year period. The operator would need to calculate the fair value of the consideration receivable by discounting the future stream of cash flows using an imputed rate in accordance with IAS 18. The operator would need to make a best estimate of the fair values of the services provided under the arrangement-operation services, repair and maintenance services (including fleet replacement where relevant). It should then allocate the total fair value of the consideration to the various services '*reference to the relative fair value of the services delivered*' (see further paras 33.68, 33.81 and 33.83). Revenue and costs would then be recognised over the operation phase in accordance with IAS 18. There is no financial asset to recognise.

Scenario 2 – Grantor gives the operator the right to charge users.

In this situation, the grantor gives the operator the right to charge users. The grantor does not provide any shortfall guarantee in fares collected from users. It would appear that the right to charge users give rise to an intangible asset because the operator bears all the demand risk and there is no minimum guarantee receivable from the grantor. As the arrangement in this scenario is identical to scenario 1 in all other respects, the question arises as to whether

维护设备等）。特许期限为 10 年，期末基础设施归还给授予方。未规定升级或扩建网络（引入新的路线等）。经营方有合同义务维护基础设施到特定服务水平，并在服务安排期末在将基础设施交还给授予方之前将其恢复至特定水平。

如上所述，此类型的安排属于 IFRIC 12 的范围，因此，此安排并不属于 IFRIC 4 的范围里。

此类安排在 IFRIC 12 未提供任何特定指引的情况下，经营方的会计处理方法阐述如下：

情形 1——授予方向经营方支付固定金额

在此情况下，授予方在整个 10 年期内每年向经营方支付一笔固定的金额。经营方将需要使用根据 IAS 18 确定估算利率对未来现金流量进行折现，以此计算应收对价的公允价值。经营方将需要对安排中所提供各项服务——运营服务、维修和维护服务（包括在相关情况下的车队替换）的公允价值进行最佳估计。然后经营方必须通过“*参考所交付服务的相对公允价值*”（参见第 33. 68 段、第 33. 81 段和第 33. 83 段），将对价的总公允价值分配至各项服务。然后根据 IAS 18 确认经营期间的收入和成本。没有需要确认的金融资产。

情形 2——授予方授予经营方向使用者收费的权利

在此情况下，授予方授予经营方向使用者收费的权利。授予方不提供从使用者处收费的任何差额担保。因为经营方承担所有需求风险而没有来自授予方的最低应收担保，向使用者收费的权利似乎会产生无形资产。此情形中的安排在所有其他方面与情形 1 的完全一样，问题在于经营方是否需要在合同开始时将现有基础设施确认为无形资产（向使用者收费的权利）。IFRIC 12 对此并未提供任何指引。

the operator would need to recognise an intangible asset for the existing infrastructure (its right to charge users) at the inception of the contract. IFRIC 12 does not provide any guidance on this point.

It would be inappropriate to recognise an intangible asset at the fair value of the expected consideration receivable from users in the absence of a construction phase with a corresponding credit to income at the contract's inception as this would be tantamount to recognising revenue in advance of performance. Furthermore, in order to recognise an intangible asset, the operator must provide consideration to the grantor. As no consideration has been provided at inception (the contract is executory and neither party has performed), we believe that in this scenario, the operator should recognise revenue from users as earned, charge operating costs as incurred and provide for its contractual obligation to maintain and restore the infrastructure in accordance with IAS 37.

Scenario 3 – Operator pays the grantor for the right to charge users

The facts are the same as in scenario 2 except that the operator is required to make cash payments to the grantor. The payment itself might be negotiated in different ways (for example, a single payment upfront, an upfront payment followed by annual payments or periodic monthly payments throughout the term of the concession arrangement). Such payments are often described in the concession agreement as 'lease rentals'.

In this situation, the payment that the operator is required to make represents a payment for acquiring the licence from the grantor to charge users of the public service. Hence, the present value of all the payments (up-front plus monthly sums) should be capitalised as the cost of the intangible asset and a corresponding obligation recognised. The liability represents the payment to be made in the future for the intangible asset acquired now. Revenue and costs will be recognised as set out in scenario 2 above.

Scenario 4 – Grantor provides a shortfall guarantee for the fares collected from users

The facts are the same as in scenario 3 except that the grantor (or a party

在合同开始时，在不存在建造阶段且缺少贷记收入时以从使用者预期应收对价的公允价值确认无形资产是不合适的，因为这无异于在提供服务之前确认收入。此外，为了确认无形资产，经营方必须向授予方支付对价。因为开始时未支付任何对价（合同为待执行合同，且任何一方尚未履行义务），我们相信在此情形下，经营方应于向使用者提供服务时确认收入、于发生费用时确认经营成本并根据 IAS 37 确认相关的维护和恢复基础设施的合同义务。

情形 3——经营方为取得向使用者收费的权利向授予方付款

除了经营方被要求向授予方支付现金外，事实与情形 2 中的相同。付款本身也许可以以不同方式协商（例如，单笔预付款、预付款随后在特许权安排期间内紧接年度付款或定期月度付款）。此类付款在特许权协议中通常被描述为“租赁租金”。

在此情况下，经营方被要求的付款代表从授予方获得向公共服务使用者收费的许可所支付的款项。因此，所有付款的现值（预付款加月支付总额）应当被资本化作为无形资产的成本，并确认相应的义务。负债代表于未来将支付的现在所获取的无形资产的对价。收入和成本将根据上述情形 2 进行确认。

情形 4——授予方对从使用者处收取的费用提供差额担保

除了授予方（或授予方的关联方）对从使用者处收取的费用提供差额担

related to the grantor) provides a shortfall guarantee for the fares collected from users.

In the example described in paragraph 33. 52 above, a shortfall guarantee has the effect of giving the operator an unconditional right to receive a certain amount of cash in consideration for construction services and so represents a financial asset. However, in this scenario the operator has not provided any construction services so the substance of the arrangement needs to be considered in order to determine whether the payments made to the grantor represent an intangible or a financial asset.

If the payment is made in order to acquire a licence to charge users, an intangible asset (together with a corresponding liability) is recognised in the same way as in scenario 3. Although the operator has a right to receive sums under the guarantee should income from users falls below a specified level, no separate financial asset should be recognised. This is because the operator has not performed under the guarantee. Contrast this with the situation in paragraph 33. 52 where the operator has provided construction services as consideration to receive the minimum guaranteed amount. Therefore, any amounts receivable under the guarantee should be recognised as revenue as the operator performs its obligations during the concession period.

On the other hand, if the payment is made in order to obtain a guaranteed level of income, a financial asset is recognised. In substance, the operator has made a loan to the grantor. The financial asset should be measured initially at fair value, which will not necessarily be equal to the present value of the payments due to the grantor. Any excess should be recognised as an intangible asset as, in substance, it represents the operator's right to earn additional income from users of the service. During the course of the concession arrangement, receipts up to the level of the guarantee are treated as settlement of the financial asset. Additional amounts collected from users are recognised as income in accordance with IAS 18. A key difference between this alternative approach and that described in the previous paragraph is that total income over the term of the arrangement will be lower. This is because a certain level of income has, in effect, been acquired rather than earned.

保外，事实与情形 3 中的相同。

在上述第 33.52 段所描述的示例中，差额担保具有赋予经营方无条件收取一定现金金额、以此作为建造服务的对价的效果，因此代表一项金融资产。然而，在此情形中，安排中经营方并未提供任何建造服务，因此应考虑安排的实质以决定向授予方的付款是代表无形资产还是金融资产。

如果支付的款项是为了获取向使用者收费的许可，则无形资产（与相应的负债一起）确认的方式与情形 3 中的相同。尽管根据担保当经营方的收入低于特定水平时，其有权获得收入，但不应确认为单独的金融资产。这是因为经营方尚未履行担保下的义务。这一情形与第 33.52 段中经营方已提供建造服务作为收取最低担保金额对价的情况不同。因此，当经营方在特许权期间履行其义务时，任何根据担保应收金额才应被确认为收入。

另一方面，如果支付的款项是为了获得担保的收入水平，则确认为金融资产。实质上，经营方向授予方发放了一笔贷款。在初始时应以公允价值计量金融资产，这不一定等于应付授予方款项的现值。任何超出金额应被确认为无形资产，由于在实质上其代表经营方从服务使用者赚取额外收入的权利。在特许权安排期间，收入达到担保水平的部分应被视为金融资产的偿付。根据 IAS 18，从使用者处收取的额外金额被确认为收入。这一替代模式和上段所述的关键不同之处在于安排期间的总收入将会较低。这是因为实际上一定水平的收入是来自于购买而非赚取。

It may be appropriate to offset the financial asset (amounts due from the grantor under the guarantee) and financial liability (amounts due to the grantor to obtain the licence/guaranteed income) under the alternative approach, where the operator has a legally enforceable right of offset and intends either to settle on a net basis or realise the asset and settle the liability simultaneously. [IAS 32 para 42]. Offsetting financial assets and liabilities is considered further in chapter 11 of IFRS Manual of Accounting – Financial Instruments.

Borrowing costs incurred by the operator

33.103 Where an operator finances the construction of an infrastructure asset, it will incur borrowing costs. IAS 23 requires borrowing costs to be recognised as an expense in the period in which they are incurred, except to the extent that they are directly attributable to the acquisition, construction or production of a qualifying asset. In the latter case the standard requires borrowing costs to be capitalised as part of the cost of the qualifying asset.

33.104 IAS 23 defines a qualifying asset as '*an asset that necessarily takes a substantial period of time to get ready for its intended use*'. For arrangements within IFRIC 12's scope, the IFRIC concluded that an intangible asset (that is, the grantor gives the operator a right to charge users of the public service in return for construction services) meets the definition of a qualifying asset of the operator because generally the licence would not be ready for use until the infrastructure was constructed or upgraded. A financial asset (that is, the grantor gives the operator a contractual right to receive cash or financial asset in return for construction services) does not meet the definition of a qualifying asset.

33.105 Therefore, in accordance with IAS 23, borrowing costs attributable to the arrangement should be recognised as an expense in the period in which they are incurred, unless the operator has a contractual right to receive an intangible asset (a right to charge users of the public service). In this case borrowing costs attributable to the arrangement are required to be capitalised during the arrangement's constructor phase. [IFRIC 12 para 22].

在替代方法下，当经营方拥有法定执行的抵销权，并旨在以净额结算或变现资产同时结算负债，抵销金融资产（应收授予方担保款）和金融负债（为获取许可/担保收入应向授予方支付的金额）可能是恰当的。[IAS 32 第42 段]。金融资产和负债的抵销在《国际财务报告准则实务指引——金融工具系列》第十一章中进一步探讨。

经营方所发生的借款费用

33.103　当经营方为基础设施资产的建造融资时，其将产生借款费用。IAS 23 要求将借款费用在发生当期确认为费用，除非该费用可直接归属于符合资本化条件的资产的收购、建造或生产。在后一种情况下，准则要求将借款费用资本化为符合条件的资产成本的组成部分。

33.104　IAS 23 将符合资本化条件的资产定义为“*需要经过相当长时间才能达到预定可使用状态的资产*”。对于 IFRIC 12 范围内的安排，由于在该基础建设直至建造或改造完毕前相关的许可并未能够使用，因此国际财务报告解释委员会认为该无形资产（即授予方给予经营方向公共服务的使用者收费以作为建造服务回报的权利）满足经营方符合资本化条件的资产的定义。金融资产（即授予方给予经营方收取现金或金融资产以作为建造服务回报的合同权利）不满足符合资本化条件的资产的定义。

33.105　因此，根据 IAS 23，除非经营方拥有获取无形资产的合同权利（向公共服务使用者收费的权利），可归属于安排的借款费用应被确认为当期费用。在取得无形资产的情况下，要求将可归属于安排的借款费用在安排的建造阶段予以资本化。[IFRIC 12 第 22 段]。

Operator recognises a financial asset

33. 106 Where an operator recognises a financial asset as consideration receivable from the grantor for the construction service provided, the operator does not capitalise borrowings costs, but expenses them as incurred. However, the operator will also record interest income during the construction and the operating periods where it classifies the financial asset as loans and receivables or available-for-sale using the effective interest method as discussed in paragraph 33. 90 above.

Operator recognises an intangible asset

33. 107 Operators that recognise an intangible asset will capitalise attributable borrowing costs as part of the intangible asset. IAS 23 provides guidance on the definition of attributable borrowing costs, how borrowing costs to be capitalised should be determined and over what period borrowing costs should be capitalised. In general, the operator will capitalise borrowing costs as they are incurred, expenditure on the asset's construction is incurred and contract activity progresses. Capitalisation should cease when the infrastructure and, therefore, the intangible asset is ready for use. Capitalisation should be suspended during extended periods in which active development is interrupted.

33. 108 Where borrowing costs are capitalised as part of the intangible asset's cost, the operator will report a different pre-tax income from another that recognises a financial asset and expenses borrowing costs during the construction phase, even if both undertake the same construction activity on the same terms. This is a normal consequence of capitalising borrowing costs instead of expensing them.

33. 109 A question arises as to what proportion of the borrowing costs incurred during the construction phase should be capitalised in circumstances where the operator recognises a financial asset and an intangible asset. The simplest way of making the allocation is to use the relative fair values of the two components (financial asset and intangible asset) into which the fair value of the construction services has been allocated. This is the method used in the example in paragraph 33. 101 above, although other reasonable bases of allocation may be used.

经营方确认金融资产

33.106　当经营方因提供建造服务而将应收授予方对价确认为金融资产时，经营方不能将借款费用资本化，应作为发生的费用。然而，如上述第33.90段所讨论的，当金融资产归类为贷款和应收款项或可供出售金融资产时，经营方也将在建造和经营阶段使用实际利率法记录利息收入。

经营方确认无形资产

33.107　确认无形资产的经营方将可归属的借款费用资本化为无形资产的组成部分。IAS 23 提供了可归属借款费用的定义和如何确定借款费用资本化及借款费用资本化的期间相关的指引。通常情况下，经营方在借款费用发生时、资产建造支出发生时和合同活动进行时将借款费用资本化。当基础设施，即无形资产达到可使用的状态时，停止资本化。当现行开发活动发生较长的中断期间，应该暂停资本化。

33.108　当借款费用被资本化为无形资产的组成部分时，即使两经营方以相同的条件承担同样的建造活动，该经营方将报告与其他在建造期间确认金融资产和将借款费用费用化的另一经营方不同的税前收入。这是借款费用资本化而没有费用化的正常结果。

33.109　问题在于，在经营方确认金融资产和无形资产的情况下，如何确定建造期间所发生借款费用应当资本化的比例。最简单的分配方法是使用这两个组成部分（金融资产和无形资产）的相对公允价值，对建造服务的公允价值进行分配。尽管其他合理的分配基础也可以使用，这是上述第 33.101 段中的示例所使用的方法。

Obligations for infrastructure maintenance during the operations phase

33. 110 Service concession arrangements generally are of long duration and the operator may have various maintenance obligations, including asset replacements and refurbishments, that it must fulfil during the operations phase before the arrangement comes to an end. A wide range of arrangements exists for the maintenance activity in connection with the infrastructure under a service concession arrangement. The arrangement's terms depend on the objectives of the grantor and the operator in negotiating the agreement, the jurisdiction and the industry sector. Typically, they require the operator to maintain the infrastructure to a specified level of service at all times and to restore the infrastructure to a specified condition before it is handed back to the grantor. As a result of these obligations, the operator may need to:

- Enhance existing infrastructure or construct new infrastructure.
- Undertake major life cycle costs (such as major overhaul).
- Replace or restore items that have been fully consumed.
- Undertake normal repairs and maintenance.

33. 111 Accordingly, where an operator has a contractual obligation it must fulfil as a condition of its licence to maintain or restore infrastructure, it must recognise and measure such obligations, except for an upgrade element, in accordance with IAS 37. [IFRIC 12 para 21]. The word 'licence' in the above paragraph is taken to refer generally to the service concession arrangement between the operator and the grantor and not to the specific licence that arises when the operator is allowed to charge users.

33. 112 This suggests that irrespective of the nature of the construction asset recognised, a financial asset (grantor pays) or an intangible asset (users pay), the operator must provide for its contractual obligations to maintain or restore the infrastructure in accordance with IAS 37 (unless the grantor agrees to reimburse the operator, see para 33. 115 below). It would appear that the above interpretation

运营阶段对基础设施维护的义务

33.110　服务特许权安排通常期限较长，而且经营方还可能有各种各样的维护义务，包括在安排结束前必须履行的资产重置和整修。在服务特许权安排中，存在基础设施相关维护活动的各种安排。安排的条款取决于授予方和经营方在协议谈判时的目标、地域和行业。通常情况下，它们要求经营方一直将基础设施维护至特定的服务水平，并在将基础设施归还授予方前将其恢复至特定的状态。由于上述义务，经营方可能需要：

- 改造现有的基础设施或建造新的基础设施。
- 承担主要寿命周期成本（如大检修）。
- 重置或恢复已被完全损耗的项目。
- 承揽常规维修和维护。

33.111　相应地，当经营方承担维护或恢复基础设施的合同义务并作为许可的条件时，除改造部分外，经营方必须根据 IAS 37 确认和计量上述义务。[IFRIC 12 第21 段]。上段中的“许可”通常被用来指经营方和授予方之间的服务特许权安排，并不是经营方被允许向使用者收费时产生的特定许可。

33.112　这意味着不论被确认的建造资产的性质是金融资产（授予方支付）或者是无形资产（使用者支付），经营方必须根据 IAS 37 对维护或恢复基础设施的合同义务进行计提（除非授予方同意偿还经营方，参见下述第 33.115 段）。上述解释似乎与 IFRIC 12 中的示例不一致，解释公告示例中类似的维护义务在金融和无形资产模型下的会计处理似乎有所不同。

does not appear to be consistent with the illustrative examples in IFRIC 12, where similar obligations for maintenance appear to have been accounted for differently under the financial and the intangible asset models.

33. 113 Under the financial asset model the contractual obligation to resurface the road is expensed when incurred. Consequently, revenue and costs are recognised as income and expenses in the period in which work is performed.

33. 114 Under the intangible asset model, the requirement to resurface the road is described as a consequence of the use of the road during the operation phase. In other words, it falls within the operator's obligation to maintain the road to a specified standard. The operator is not specifically remunerated for its maintenance activities. Consequently, such maintenance obligations are recognised and measured in accordance with IAS 37, that is, at the best estimate of the expenditure required to settle the present obligation at the balance sheet date. However, enhancement expenditure goes beyond this. If the operator agrees to incur enhancement expenditure as well, this suggests that the service concession has as inherent value that is not contingent on the use of the infrastructure (see para 33. 117 below).

33. 115 The differences between the two sets of circumstances described above are subtle. The appropriate accounting treatment for maintenance obligations will depend on the obligations' precise nature, terms and circumstances, which would vary from contract to contract and should not be affected by the nature of the infrastructure asset recognised (a financial asset or an intangible asset). Therefore, where the grantor agrees to reimburse major expenditure necessary to maintain the infrastructure, it should be treated as a revenue generating activity and revenue and costs should be recognised when the expenditure is undertaken. Where the grantor is not required to reimburse such expenditure, a provision should be made as the infrastructure is consumed.

Major refurbishments and renewals

33. 116 A considerable amount of judgement is needed in determining the timing and recognition of unavoidable obligations that the operator owes to the grantor in

33.113 在金融资产模型下，公路重铺路面的合同义务在发生时进行费用化。因此，收入和成本在履行工作期间确认为收入和费用。

33.114 在无形资产模型下，公路重铺路面的要求被描述成经营期间公路使用的结果。换言之，维护公路到特定的标准属于经营方的义务。经营方不会因为其维护活动而特别获得报酬。因此，对此类维护义务需根据 IAS 37 进行确认和计量，即在资产负债表日对所要求的支出进行最佳估计以结算现有义务。然而，改造支出不仅限于此。如果经营方也同意发生改造支出，这意味着服务特许权存在着不取决于基础设施使用的内在价值（参见下述第 33.117 段）。

33.115 上述两组情况之间的差异是微妙的。维护义务恰当的会计处理将取决于义务的确切性质、条款和情况，其因合同而异，而不应该受所确认的基础设施资产的性质（金融资产或无形资产）所影响。因此，当授予方同意偿付基础设施维护所必须的重大支出的情况下，它应该被视为产生收入的活动，并在费用支出时确认收入和成本。当不要求授予方偿付上述支出时，随着基础设施的消耗应计提准备。

重大整修和翻新

33.116 当经营方对授予方在基础设施上承担不可避免的义务时，需要进行大量的判断以确定其时点和确认问题。因此，当主体有义务承担重大支出

respect of the infrastructure. Therefore, where an entity has an obligation to undertake major expenditure (such major refurbishments and renewals subject to cyclic repair), a provision should be recognised; the obligating event being the consumption or use of the infrastructure asset up to the balance sheet date. The provision would be recognised under IAS 37 at the best estimate of the amount of the expenditure expected to be incurred to perform the major overhaul or restoration work, discounted using a rate that reflects the time value of money and the risks involved-(see also table 6 in the example in para 33. 101 above). Other life-cycle expenditure, such as normal repairs and maintenance costs are likely to be executory in nature and would be recognised when incurred. [IFRIC 12 para BC 68].

33. 116. 1 The facts and circumstances might indicate that at inception of the service concession arrangement an operator assumes liabilities for existing maintenance work as consideration for the acquired rights. In this case, the operator should recognise a liability only for those obligations to carry out specific work that existed at the date of acquisition, recognising the corresponding debit as part of the cost of the intangible asset. However, it would not be appropriate to recognise a liability in respect of obligations to enhance or upgrade the infrastructure or construct new infrastructure as explained in the following paragraph.

Enhancement or new infrastructure (upgrade)

33. 117 A service concession arrangement's terms may require the operator to enhance or upgrade existing infrastructure (that would extend its life or capacity) or construct new infrastructure (for example, adding a new hospital wing or adding a new lane to an existing road) during the operation phase. The operator is not required to recognise any provision in advance of the upgrade as noted in paragraph 33. 111 above. [IFRIC 12 para 21]. Instead, the operator recognises revenue, being the fair value of such expenditure, in accordance with IAS 11 as the upgrade activity progresses and expenditure is incurred. [IFRIC 12 para 14].

33. 118 To the extent that the operator has the right to recover the upgrade costs, including the margin, through the amount receivable from the grantor over the life

（如重大整修和定期翻新）时，应确认准备；义务事项是直到资产负债表日基础设施的消耗或使用。该准备根据 IAS 37 以最佳估计履行重大检修或恢复工作预计发生的支出的金额来确认，并使用反映货币时间价值和相关风险的利率进行折现（同时参见上述第 33.101 中的示例）。其他寿命周期内的支出，如常规维修和维护成本可能是待执行性质的，在发生时确认。[IFRIC 12 BC 第 68 段]。

33.116.1　事实和情况可能表明在服务特许权安排开始时，经营方承担现有维护工作的负债以此作为获得权利的对价。在这一情况下，经营方应仅确认在收购日存在的实施特定工作而产生的负债，确认相应的借方作为无形资产成本的组成部分。然而，如下段所述，针对基础设施改造或升级或新基础设施建造相关义务而确认负债并不恰当。

改造或新的基础设施（升级）

33.117　服务特许权安排的条款可能要求经营方在运营阶段改造或升级现有的基础设施（延长其寿命或扩展其性能）或建造新的基础设施（例如，增建新的医院翼楼或者在现有公路上增加新的车道）。如上述第 33.111 段中所提及，不要求经营方在升级之前提前确认任何准备。[IFRIC 12 第 21 段]。相反，经营方应根据 IAS 11，随着升级活动的开展和支出的发生，以此类支出的公允价值确认收入。[IFRIC 12 第 14 段]。

33.118　当经营方有权通过在特许周期内从授予方的应收款项中收回升级成本包括毛利时，被确认为收入的升级公允价值应加入到金融资产中。同样地，

of the concession, the fair value of the upgrade that is recognised as revenue is added to the financial asset. Similarly, to the extent that the operator has been given the right to charge users, the fair value of the expenditure will be recognised as an intangible asset or added to any intangible asset recognised previously. The increase in the value of the intangible asset is not regarded as a revaluation of any existing intangible asset, but simply reflects the fact that the operator will generate additional revenue from new users of the hospital wing or the new lane. Where the operator is accounting for the concession arrangement under the intangible asset model, but the arrangement provides reimbursement by the grantor for a proportion of any upgrade expenditure to be incurred at a future date, a proportion of the revenue recognised as upgrade activity progresses will be allocated to the amount receivable from the grantor and the balance will be recognised as an intangible asset.

Items provided to the operator by the grantor

33.119 A public sector organisation (grantor) may contribute infrastructure assets (for example, land and/or other assets) to the operator. Where such infrastructure assets are required for the operator to carry out its obligations under the contract, they remain the grantor's property and are not recognised as the operator's assets (see para 33.37 above).

33.120 Sometimes, the grantor may provide other items to the operator that the operator can keep or deal with as it wishes. They are recognised as the operator's assets, measured at fair value on initial recognition. The operator should record a liability in respect of the unfulfilled obligations it has assumed in exchange for the assets. [IFRIC 12 para 27].

33.121 Assets that the operator can keep or deal with as it wishes and which form part of the consideration payable by the grantor for the services rendered are not regarded as government grants as defined in IAS 20. This is because if such assets are part of the consideration payable by the grantor on an arm's length basis for the operator's services, they are not 'assistance'. Therefore, they fail to meet the definition of a government grant and are scoped out of IAS 20.

当经营方被给予向使用者收费的权利时，支出的公允价值将被确认为无形资产或加入到之前确认的任何无形资产中。无形资产价值的增加不被视为任何现有无形资产的重估，但仅反映经营方将从医院翼楼或新车道的使用者处产生额外收入的权利。当经营方在无形资产模型下核算特许权安排时，但安排规定授予方进行偿付部分在未来日期将要发生的任何升级支出，升级活动进度收入的一部分将被分配至应收授予方款项，并将余额确认为无形资产。

由授予方提供给经营方的项目

33.119　公共部门组织（授予方）可能提供基础设施资产（例如，土地和/或其他资产）给经营方。当经营方根据合同需要使用此类基础设施资产履行其义务时，它们仍是授予方的资产，并不被确认为经营方的资产（参见上述第33.37段）。

33.120　授予方有时可能向经营方提供其他项目，经营方可根据自身意愿保留或进行处理。它们被确认为经营方的资产，以公允价值作初始计量。经营方应记录其为交换该资产而承担的未履行义务相关的负债。［IFRIC 12 第27段］。

33.121　经营方可根据自身意愿保留或处理的资产作为授予方为所交付的服务应付对价的组成部分而非 IAS 20 下的政府补助。这是因为如果上述资产在经营方服务公平交易的基础上是授予方应付对价的组成部分，它们则不是“援助”。因此，它们不能满足政府援助的定义，超出了 IAS 20 的范围。

33.121.1 A question arises as to whether IFRIC 18 has any impact on infrastructure that is transferred from the grantor to the operator in a service concession arrangement. Paragraph 7 of IFRIC 18 makes it clear that the interpretation does not apply to infrastructure used in a service concession arrangement within the scope of IFRIC 12. This scope exclusion makes sense since under IFRIC 18 an asset would be recognised by the entity only when it controls the asset transferred from the customer. This is not the case under a service concession arrangement under IFRIC 12, where control of the transferred infrastructure is retained by the grantor/customer. However, there may be circumstances where the grantor transfers control of the asset to the operator that the operator can keep or deal with as it pleases. As discussed above such assets are recognised as the operator's asset at fair value, which is consistent with the treatment set out in IFRIC 18.

Example – Treatment of items provided by the grantor

A public sector organisation contributes land to a private sector operator on which the operator is required to build a property to be used in a public-to-private service concession arrangement. The construction is expected to take two years to complete. The fair values of the construction activity in accordance with IAS 11 are C12m in year 1 and C8m in year 2. The grantor agrees that once the building on the new site is completed at the end of year 2, a nearby building owned by the grantor will be vacated and handed to the operator to keep or sell. The fair value of the old building at the date of inception of the contract is C5m, which is also its fair value at the handover date at the end of year 2.

Scenario 1 – The operator recognises a financial asset

During the period of construction, the operator recognises construction revenue of C20m and a financial asset of C20m. At the end of year 2, after completion of the construction activity, the operator receives a property worth C5m, which it is entitled to keep or sell, as additional consideration. The operator will record the construction revenue and the consideration received from the grantor as follows:

33.121.1 有一问题值得探讨，IFRIC 18 是否对服务特许权安排中从授予方转移至经营方的基础设施有任何影响。IFRIC 18 第 7 段明确指出，解释并不适用于 IFRIC 12 范围中使用于服务特许权安排中的基础设施。这一范围排除言之有理，因为根据 IFRIC 18，只有当主体控制从客户处转移出的资产时才能进行确认。根据 IFRIC 12 在服务特许权安排中并非如此，转移的基础设施控制权仍由授予方/客户保留。然而，可能在有的情况下，授予方将资产的控制权转移至经营方，而经营方可根据自身意愿保留或进行处置。如上所讨论，此类资产以其公允价值被确认为经营方的资产，这与 IFRIC 18 中所阐述的处理方法相一致。

示例——由授予方提供的项目的处理

公共部门组织向私营部门经营方提供了一块土地，经营方需要在土地上建造不动产并用于公共/私营服务特许权安排。建造预期需要两年完工。根据 IAS 11，建造活动的公允价值在第 1 年为 1,200 万元，在第 2 年为 800 万元。授予方同意一旦新址上的建筑在第 2 年年末完工，由授予方所有的附近的一幢建筑将腾空交付经营方保管或出售。在合同开始时旧建筑的公允价值为 500 万元，这也是第 2 年年末交接当日的公允价值。

情形 1——经营方确认金融资产

在建造期间，经营方确认 2,000 万元的建造收入和 2,000 万元的金融资产。在第 2 年年末，在建造活动完工以后，经营方获得价值为 500 万元的不动产，并有权将其保留或者出售，作为额外的对价。经营方将记录建造收入和从授予方处获得的对价如下：

	Dr	Cr
Year 1		
Financial asset	12	
Construction revenue		12

The operator recognises construction revenue on the percentage of completion basis in accordance with IAS 11.

Year 2		
Financial asset	8	
Construction revenue		8

The operator recognises construction revenue on the percentage of completion basis in accordance with IAS 11. For the purposes of this example, the recognition of finance income in year 2 is ignored.

It will be apparent from the arrangement's terms whether the non-cash consideration received by the operator represents consideration received for construction services or for services to be performed in the future. Where the former applies, it would be appropriate for the operator to set-off the fair value of the land of C5m against the financial asset of C20m in year 2. Where the latter applies, the operator will recognise deferred income of C5m, which will be released to revenue as performance is completed. In either situation, the operator treats the land as an owned asset and accounts for it in accordance with IAS 16.

Scenario 2 – The operator recognises an intangible asset

In this scenario, the grantor gives the operator alicence to charge users of the public service. As in scenario 1, the operator will recognise revenue of C20m as construction services are provided over a two year period. At the end of

	借	贷
第 1 年		
金融资产	12	
建造收入		12

经营方根据 IAS 11 基于完工百分比确认建造收入。

第 2 年		
金融资产	8	
建造收入		8

经营方根据 IAS 11 基于完工百分比确认建造收入。就此示例而言，忽略第 2 年融资收益的确认。

从安排的条款中可以明显地看出经营方获得的非现金对价是代表建造服务还是未来待履行服务的应收对价。如果适用前者，经营方在第 2 年以 500 万元土地的公允价值抵销 2,000 万元金融资产是恰当的。如果适用后者，经营方将确认 500 万元的递延收入，在工作完成之后将被确认为收入。在上述任一情况下，经营方将土地视为自有资产，并根据 IAS 16 进行会计处理。

情形 2——经营方确认无形资产

在此情形中，授予方给予经营方向公共服务的使用者收费的许可。如情形 1 中，在提供建造服务的两年内经营方将确认 2,000 万元的收入。在第 2 年年末，经营方收到价值 500 万元的不动产作为建造服务的部分付

year 2, the operator receives property worth C5m as partial payment for the construction services as well as intangible asset worth C15m (a licence to charge users).

As the construction activity progresses, it is not clear how the fair value of the land of C5m, which is treated as partial payment for the construction services, should be recognised in years 1 and 2.

One approach would be to adopt a pro-rata approach and recognise a non-cash receivable in year 1 and 2. The non-cash receivable would be derecognised and replaced by property, plant and equipment when it is settled by the receipt of land at the end of year 2. A *pro rata* approach is acceptable because IAS 18 states that when goods are delivered or services are rendered (in this situation construction services) in exchange for dissimilar goods or services (tangible asset and an intangible asset), the exchange is regarded as a transaction that gives rise to revenue. [IAS 18 para 12]. Under this approach, the accounting entries would be as follows:

	Dr	Cr
Year 1		
Non-cash receivable	3	
Intangible asset	9	
Construction revenue		12

The operator recognises construction revenue on the percentage of completion basis in accordance with IAS 11 and records consideration receivable as indicated above.

Year 2		
Non-cash receivable	2	
Intangible asset	6	
Construction revenue		8

款和价值 1,500 万元的无形资产（向使用者收费的许可）。

建造活动进行中，被作为建造服务部分价款的公允价值为 500 万元的土地应如何在第 1 年和第 2 年确认并不清楚。

一种办法是采用比例法来确认第 1 年和第 2 年的非现金应收款项。在第 2 年年末当收到土地作为对非现金应收款项的结算时，应终止确认非现金应收款项并由不动产、工厂和设备代替。比例法是可以接受的，因为 IAS 18 指出，当交付货物或提供服务时（在这一情况下为建造服务）以不同的货物或服务（有形资产和无形资产）作交换，该交换被视为产生收入的交易。［IAS 18 第 12 段］。在这一方法下，会计分录如下：

	借	贷
第 1 年		
非现金应收款项	3	
无形资产	9	
建造收入		12

经营方根据 IAS 11 基于完工百分比确认建造收入，并按上述所示，对应记录应收对价。

第 2 年		
非现金应收款	2	
无形资产	6	
建造收入		8

The operator recognises construction revenue on the percentage of completion basis in accordance with IAS 11 and records consideration receivable as indicated above.

Property, plant and equipment	5	
Non-cash receivable		5

The operator derecognises the non-cash receivable and recognises the property as settlement for the receivable. The operator treats the fixed asset as owned asset and accounts for it in accordance with IAS 16. The intangible asset of C15m is amortised over the life of the arrangement.

Another approach would be to record the asset when it is received, that is, when construction is completed and treat it as partial payment of the total consideration as shown below.

	Dr	Cr
Year 1		
Intangible asset	12	
Construction revenue		12

The operator recognises construction revenue on the percentage of completion basis in accordance with IAS 11.

Year 2		
Property plant and equipment	5	
Intangible asset	3	
Construction revenue		8

经营方根据 IAS 11 基于完工百分比确认建造收入，并按上述所示，对应记录应收对价。

不动产、工厂和设备	5	
非现金应收款项		5

经营方终止确认非现金应收款项，并确认不动产作为对应收款项的结算。经营方将固定资产作为自有资产，并根据 IAS 16 进行会计核算。1,500 万元的无形资产在安排的有效期内摊销。

另一种方法是在接收资产时确认，即当建造完工时作为总对价的部分价款，如下所示：

	借	贷
第 1 年		
无形资产	12	
建造收入		12

经营方根据 IAS 11 基于完工百分比确认建造收入。

第 2 年		
不动产、工厂和设备	5	
无形资产	3	
建造收入		8

The operator recognises construction revenue on the percentage of completion basis in accordance with IAS 11. In addition, it receives a non-cash asset of C5m as partial payment for providing construction services to the operator. In other words, at the end of year 2, the operator receives a tangible asset of C5m and an intangible asset (a licence to charge users) of C15m as consideration for providing construction services of C20m.

There is no deferred revenue in this scenario as the operator has already performed its obligations to the grantor in advance of consideration receivable. In other words, the intangible asset of C15m represents the operator's right to receive revenue from the users. The intangible asset is amortised as those revenues are earned.

The choice of approach is important as the proportion of borrowings costs capitalised in years 1 and 2 will differ between the two approaches giving rise to different pre-tax numbers in those years, although total borrowing costs incurred during the two year construction period would be the same. An operator will choose the one that is most appropriate to its circumstances.

Disclosure requirements

General

33.122 There are no specific disclosure requirements in IFRIC 12. The disclosure requirements relating to service concession arrangements are contained in SIC 29, which was issued in December 2001. On the publication of IFRIC 12, the IFRIC made some minor changes to SIC 29. It amended the title and replaced the terms 'concession provider' and 'concession operator' with 'grantor' and 'operator' respectively. It also added a couple of new disclosure requirements, but left the existing disclosure requirements of SIC 29 intact. Not all service concession arrangements are within IFRIC 12's scope.

33.123 SIC 29 states that the common characteristic of all service concession arrangements is that the operator both receives a right and incurs an obligation to provide public services. The disclosure requirements are centred round this

经营方根据 IAS 11 基于完工百分比确认建造收入。另外，经营方获得 500 万元的非现金资产作为经营方提供建造服务的部分价款。换言之，在第 2 年年末，经营方收取 500 万元的有形资产和无形资产（向使用者收费的许可）作为提供 2,000 万元建造服务的对价。

因为经营方已在收取对价前履行了对授予方的义务，因此在此情形中并没有递延收入。换言之，1,500 万元的无形资产代表经营方从使用者处取得收入的权利。无形资产在取得收入的期间摊销。

方法的选择很重要，因为尽管在两年建造期间内发生的借款费用相同，但是这两种方法将会使得在第 1 年和第 2 年借款费用资本化的比例不同，从而导致不同的税前金额。经营方将会选择最适合其情况的方法。

披露要求

一般原则

33.122　IFRIC 12 中没有特定的披露要求。2001 年 12 月发布的 SIC 29 中包含了特许服务权安排相关的披露要求。在 IFRIC 12 发布时，国际财务报告解释委员会对 SIC 29 进行了微小的改动。它修改了标题，并以“授予方”和“经营方”分别替代了“特许权提供方”和“特许权经营方”这两个术语。此外，它还增加了一些新的披露要求，但是完整地保留了 SIC 29 中的现有披露要求。不是所有的特许服务权安排都在 IFRIC 12 地的范围之内。

33.123　SIC 29 指出，所有特许服务权安排的共同特征是经营方既获得一项权利，又产生一项提供公共服务的义务。尽管 IFRIC 12 仅适用于经营方的会计处理，披露要求以此为中心，既适用于授予方又适用于经营方。

requirement and apply to both the grantor and the operator, although IFRIC 12 only applies to accounting by the operator.

33.124 SIC 29's disclosure requirements are in addition to those in other standards that may apply to certain aspects of service concession arrangements, such as IAS 16, IAS 17 and IAS 38. IFRS 7 also applies where an operator recognises a financial asset. [IFRIC 12 para 23].

Specific disclosures

33.125 All aspects of a service concession arrangement should be considered in determining the appropriate disclosure in the notes. The specific disclosures that should be made in each period are as follows:

- A description of the arrangement.
- Significant terms of the arrangement that may affect the amount, timing and certainty of future cash flows (for example, the period of the concession, re-pricing dates and the basis upon which re-pricing or re-negotiation is determined).
- The nature and extent (for example, quantity, time period or amount as appropriate) of:
  - rights to use specified assets;
  - obligations to provide or rights to expect provision of services;
  - obligations to acquire or build items of property, plant and equipment;
  - obligations to deliver or rights to receive specified assets at the end of the concession period;
  - renewal and termination options; and
  - other rights and obligations (for example, major overhauls).
- Changes in the arrangement occurring during the period.
- How the service arrangement has been classified.

33.124　SIC 29 的披露要求是对其他可能适用于特许服务权安排某些方面的其他准则（如 IAS 16、IAS 17 和 IAS 38）中的披露要求的补充。此外，在经营方确认金融资产的情况下，IFRS 7 也适用。[IFRIC 12 第 23 段]。

特定披露

33.125　在确定在附注中的恰当披露时，应当考虑一项特许服务权安排的所有方面。在每个期间所做的特定披露如下：

- 对安排的描述。
- 可能影响未来现金流量金额、时间和确定性的重要的安排条款（例如，特许权期间、重定价的日期和确定重定价或重新协商的基础）。
- 如下事项的性质和范围（例如，数量、期间或金额（视情况而定））：
  - 使用指定资产的权利；
  - 提供服务的义务或期望服务提供的权利；
  - 购买或建造不动产、工厂和设备项目的义务；
  - 在特许权期末交付指定资产的义务或取得指定资产的权利；
  - 续约和终止选择权；以及
  - 其他权利和义务（例如，大修）。
- 在期间发生的安排变更。
- 如何对服务安排进行分类。

[SIC 29 para 6].

33. 126 An operator should also disclose the amount of the revenue and profits or losses recognised in the period on exchanging construction services for a financial asset or an intangible asset. [SIC 29 para 6A].

33. 127 The above disclosures should be provided individually for each service concession arrangement or in aggregate for each class of service concession arrangements. A class is a grouping of service concession arrangements involving services of a similar nature (for example, toll collections, telecommunications and water treatment services). [SIC 29 para 7].

33. 128 The following tables provide comprehensive examples of entities making disclosures in accordance with IFRIC 12.

Table 33. 1 – IFRIC 12, accounting policies, SIC 29, disclosure of various service concessions arrangements

Veolia Environnement SA – Annual Report – 31 December 2011

1 Accounting principles and methods (extract)

See Note 1. 20 on Service concession arrangements.

1. 20 Description of Group concession activities

In the course of its business, Veolia Environnement provides collective services (distribution of drinking water and heating, passenger transport network, household waste collection, etc.) to local authorities in return for a remuneration based on services rendered.

These collective services (also known as services of general interest or general economic interest or public services) are generally managed by Veolia Environnement under contracts entered into at the request of public bodies which retain control thereof.

Concession arrangements involve the transfer of operating rights for a limited period, under the control of the local authority, using dedicated installations built by Veolia Environnement, or made available to it for a fee or nil consideration:

- These contracts define 'public service obligations' in return for remuneration. The remuneration is based on operating conditions, continuity of service, price rules and obligations with respect to the maintenance/replacement of installations. The contract determines the conditions for the transfer of installations to the local authority or a successor at its term;

[SIC 29 第 6 段]。

33.126　经营方也应披露在以建造服务交换金融资产或无形资产的期间所确认的收入和损益。[SIC 29 第 6A 段]。

33.127　上述披露应按每项特许服务权安排分别披露，或者按每类特许服务权安排合并披露。一类是指一组涉及类似性质服务的特许服务权安排（例如，征收通行费、通讯和水处理服务）。[SIC 29 第 7 段]。

33.128　下列表格提供了主体依据 IFRIC 12 进行披露的综合示例。

表 33.1——IFRIC 12、会计政策、SIC 29、各种特许服务权安排的披露

Veolia 环境 SA——年报——2011 年 12 月 31 日

1 会计原则和方法（摘要）

参见附注 1.20 的特许服务权安排。

1.20 集团特许权业务活动描述

在其业务过程中，Veolia 环境公司向地方当局提供综合服务（饮用水配送和供暖、客运网络、家庭垃圾收集等）并基于所提供的服务收取报酬作为回报。

这些综合服务（也称为一般利益或者一般经济利益服务，或者公共服务）通常由 Veolia 环境公司按公共机构要求签订的合同进行管理，而上述公共机构保留对这些活动的控制。

特许权安排涉及在有限的期间内转移由地方当局控制的经营权、采用 Veolia 环境公司建造的或者能够以收费或零对价的形式使用的专用设施。

- 这些合同定义“公共服务义务”，以报酬作为回报。报酬基于经营条件、服务持续性、价格规则，以及对于设施的维护/重置相关的义务而定。合同在其条款中确定将设施移交给地方当局或者继任者的条件；

Con.

- Veolia Environnement can, in certain cases, be responsible for a given service as it holds the service support network (water/heat distribution network, water treatment network). Such situations are the result of full or partial privatizations. Provisions impose public service obligations and the means by which the local authority may recover control of the concession holder.

These contracts generally include price review clauses. These clauses are mainly based on cost trends, inflation, changes in tax and/or other legislation and occasionally on changes in volumes and/or the occurrence of specific events changing the profitability of the contract.

In addition, the Group generally assumes a contractual obligation to maintain and repair facilities managed under public service contracts. The resulting maintenance and repair costs are analyzed in accordance with IAS 37 on provisions and, where appropriate, a provision for contractual commitments is recorded in respect of commitments resulting from delays in the performance of work.

The nature and extent of the Group's rights and obligations under these different contracts differ according to the public services rendered by the different Group divisions.

The accounting treatment is disclosed in Notes 6 and 11.

Water

Veolia Environnement manages municipal drinking water and/or waste water services. These services encompass all or part of the water cycle (extraction from natural sources, treatment, storage and distribution followed by collection and treatment of waste water and release into the environment).

In France, these services are primarily rendered under public service delegation 'affermage' contracts with a term of 8 to 20 years. They concern the production and distribution of drinking water and/or the collection and treatment of waste water. They use specific assets, such as distribution or wastewater treatment networks and drinking water or wastewater treatment plants, which are generally provided by the concession grantor and returned to it at the end of the contract.

Abroad, Veolia Environnement renders its services under contracts which reflect local legislation, the economic situation of the country and the investment needs of each partner.

These contracts are generally concession arrangements, service contracts or O&M (Operate & Manage) and BOT contracts with an average term of between 7 and 40 years, and sometimes longer.

续表

• 在某些情况下，Veolia 环境公司能够负责提供指定的服务是因为它拥有服务支持网络（供水/供暖网络、水处理网络）。这种情况是全部或部分私有化的结果。条款强加了公共服务义务及地方当局可以恢复对特许权持有人的控制的方式。 这些合同通常包括价格复核条款。这些条款主要基于成本趋势、通货膨胀、税务和/或其他法规变化及有时量的改变/或改变合同盈利能力的特定事项的发生。 此外，集团通常承担维护和维修根据公共服务合同所管理的设施的合同义务。所产生的维护和维修成本在计提准备时根据 IAS 37 进行分析，且在恰当的时候，针对由于工作执行延误而产生的承诺记录一项合同承诺准备。 这些不同的合同所规定的集团的权利和义务的性质和范围根据集团不同部门所提供的公共服务而异。 会计处理在附注 6 和附注 11 中披露。 **水资源** Veolia 环境公司管理着市政饮用水和/或污水服务。这些服务涵盖所有或部分水循环（从自然资源采集、处理、存储和配送，及之后的污水收集、处理和返还给环境）。 在法国，这些服务主要根据公共服务授权“租赁”合同提供，合同期限为 8—20 年。它们涉及饮用水的生产和配送和/或污水的收集和处理。它们使用特定资产，如配送或污水处理网络和饮用水或污水处理厂，这些通常由特许权授予方提供，并在合同终止时返还给授予方。 在国外，Veolia 环境公司根据反映了当地法规、国家经济情况和各合作方的投资需求的合同提供服务。 这些合同通常是特许权安排、服务合同，或者 O&M（运营和管理）及 BOT（建造 - 运营 - 转移）合同，平均期限为 7—40 年，有时更长。

Con.

Contracts can also be entered into with public entities in which Veolia Environnement purchased an interest on their partial privatization. The profitability of these contracts is not fundamentally different from other contracts, but operations are based on a partnership agreement with the local authority.

Environmental Services

Both in France and abroad, the main concession arrangements entered into by Veolia Environnement concern the treatment and recovery of waste in sorting units, storage and incineration. These contracts have an average term of 18 to 30 years.

Energy Services

Veolia Environnement has developed a range of energy management activities: heating and cooling networks, thermal and multi-technical services, industrial utilities, installation and maintenance of production equipment, integration services for the comprehensive management of buildings and electrical services on public roadways.

The main contracts concern the management of heating and air-conditioning networks under urban concessions or on behalf of local authorities.

In Eastern Europe, Veolia Environnement's Energy Services division provides services under mixed partial privatizations or through public private partnerships with local authorities responsible for the production and distribution of thermal energy.

Veolia Environnement's Transportation Division provides passenger transport services on behalf of local, regional and national public authorities.

Veolia Environnement primarily provides these services in France and abroad under service contracts comprising public service obligations (as per EU terminology), with terms of 7 to 15 years.

Accounting for service concession arrangements

Concession arrangements are recognized in accordance with IFRIC 12, *Service Concession Arrangements.*

续表

此外，Veolia 环境公司还可与公共主体签订合同购买部分私有化权益。这些合同的盈利能力与其他合同没有根本不同，但其运营基于与地方当局的合伙协议。

环境服务

Veolia 环境公司在法国和国外签订的主要的特许权安排都涉及分类单元废弃物的处理和回收利用、存储和焚化。这些合同的平均期限为 18—30 年。

能源服务

Veolia 环境公司开发了一系列的能源管理业务活动：供暖和制冷网络、热源和综合技术服务、工业类公用事业、生产设备的安装和维护、建筑物综合管理集成服务以及公共道路的电力服务。

主要的合同根据城市特许权或代表地方当局涉及供暖和空调网络的管理。

在东欧，Veolia 环境公司的能源服务部门根据混合部分私有化或通过与地方当局建立的负责热能生产和配送的公私合作关系提供服务。

Veolia 环境公司的运输部门代表当地、地区和全国公共当局提供客运服务。

Veolia 环境公司主要根据包括公共服务义务（根据欧盟术语）的服务合同在法国和国外提供这些服务，期限为 7—15 年。

特许服务权安排的会计处理

特许权安排依据《国际财务报告解释公告第 12 号——特许服务权安排》进行确认。

Con.

A substantial portion of the Group's assets is used within the framework of concession or affermage contracts granted by public sector customers (' grantors ') and/or by concession companies purchased by the Group on full or partial privatization. The characteristics of these contracts vary significantly depending on the country and activity concerned.

Nonetheless, they generally provide, directly or indirectly, for customer involvement in the determination of the service and its remuneration, and the return of the assets necessary to the performance of the service at the end of the contract.

IFRIC 12 is applicable to concession arrangements comprising a public service obligation and satisfying all of the following criteria:

- the concession grantor controls or regulates the services to be provided by the operator using the asset, the infrastructure, the beneficiaries of the services and prices applied;
- the grantor controls the significant residual interest in the infrastructure at the end of the term of the arrangement.

Pursuant to IFRIC 12, such infrastructures are not recognized in assets of the operator as property, plant and equipment but in financial assets (" financial asset model ") and/or intangible assets (" intangible asset model ") depending on the remuneration commitments given by the grantor.

1. 20. 1 Financial asset model

The financial asset model applies when the operator has an unconditional right to receive cash or another financial asset from the grantor in remuneration for concession services.

In the case of concession services, the operator has such an unconditional right if the grantor contractually guarantees the payment of:

- amounts specified or determined in the contract or
- the shortfall, if any, between amounts received from users of the public service and amounts specified or determined in the contract.

Financial assets resulting from the application of IFRIC 12 are recorded in the Consolidated Statement of Financial Position under the heading "Operating financial assets" and recognized at amortized cost.

续表

相当大部分的集团资产在公共部门客户（“授予方”）授予的特许权或租赁合同框架内使用和/或由集团通过全部或部分私有化收购的特许权公司使用。这些合同的特征因国家和涉及的业务活动差异很大。 尽管如此，它们通常直接或间接允许客户参与对服务及报酬和合同终止时服务执行必需资产的归还的决定。 IFRIC 12 适用于包含公共服务义务并满足下列所有条件的特许权安排： • 特许权授予方控制或管制经营方使用资产所提供的服务、基础设施、服务的对象和适用的价格； • 在安排期末，授予方控制基础设施的重大剩余权益。 根据 IFRIC 12，这样的基础设施不作为经营方确认为不动产、工厂和设备的资产，而应根据授予方所给予的报酬承诺，确认为金融资产（“金融资产模式”）和/或无形资产（“无形资产模式”）。 **1.20.1 金融资产模式** 当经营方有权无条件从授予方处获得现金或其他金融资产作为特许服务权的报酬时，适用金融资产模式。 在特许服务权的情况下，如果授予方根据合同规定担保如下付款，则经营方拥有一项无条件权利： • 合同中指定或者确定的金额，或者 • 从公共服务使用者收取的金额与合同中指定或确定的金额之间的差额（如有）。 因应用 IFRIC 12 而产生的金融资产在合并财务状况表中记录为“经营性金融资产”，并以摊余成本确认。

Con.

Unless otherwise indicated in the contract, the effective interest rate is equal to the weighted average cost of capital of the entities carrying the assets concerned.

Pursuant to IAS 39, an impairment loss is recognized if the carrying amount of these assets exceeds the present value of future cash flows discounted at the initial EIR.

The portion falling due within less than one year is presented in "Current operating financial assets", while the portion falling due within more than one year is presented in the non-current heading.

Revenue associated with this financial model includes:

- revenue recorded on a completion basis, in the case of construction operating financial assets (in accordance with IAS 11);
- the remuneration of the operating financial asset recorded in Revenue from operating financial assets (excluding principal payments);
- service remuneration.

1.20.2 Intangible asset model

The intangible asset model applies where the operator is paid by the users or where the concession grantor has not provided a contractual guarantee in respect of the recoverable amount. The intangible asset corresponds to the right granted by the concession grantor to the operator to charge users of the public service in remuneration of concession services.

Intangible assets resulting from the application of IFRIC 12 are recorded in the Consolidated Statement of Financial Position under the heading 'Concession intangible assets' and are amortized, generally on a straight-line basis, over the contract term.

Under the intangible asset model, Revenue includes:

- revenue recorded on a completion basis for assets and infrastructure under construction (in accordance with IAS 11);
- service remuneration.

1.20.3 Mixed or bifurcation model

The choice of the financial asset or intangible asset model depends on the existence of payment guarantees granted by the concession grantor.

续表

除非合同中另有说明，实际利率等于相关资产持有主体的资本加权平均成本。

依据 IAS 39，如果这些资产的账面价值超过未来现金流量以初始实际利率折现后的现值，则确认减值损失。

不足一年的部分列报为“流动经营性金融资产”，而超过一年的部分列报为非流动。

与此金融资产模式相关的收入包括：

- 如果建造经营性金融资产，根据完工情况记录的收入（根据 IAS 11）；
- 记录于经营性金融资产收入中的经营性金融资产报酬（不包括本金付款）；
- 服务报酬。

1.20.2 无形资产模式

当经营方由使用者付款或特许权授予方未提供与可回收金额相关的合同担保时，适用于无形资产模式。无形资产相当于特许权授予方向经营方授予的向公共服务的使用者收费以作为特许服务的报酬的权利。

因应用 IFRIC 12 而产生的无形资产在合并财务状况表中记录为“特许权无形资产”，并在合同期限内通常以直线法摊销。

在无形资产模式之下，收入包括：

- 根据完工情况记录的建造中的资产和基础设施的收入（根据 IAS 11）；
- 服务报酬。

1.20.3 混合或分叉模式

金融资产或无形资产模式取决于是否存在由特许权授予方提供的付款担保。

Con.

However, certain contracts may include a payment commitment on the part of the concession grantor covering only part of the investment, with the balance covered by royalties charged to users.

Where this is the case, the investment amount guaranteed by the concession grantor is recognized under the financial asset model and the residual balance is recognized under the intangible asset model.

Table 33.2 – IFRIC 12, accounting policies, SIC 29, disclosure of various service concessions arrangements

Bilfinger Berger SE – Annual report – 31 December 2011

6. Significant accounting policies (extract)

Revenue from construction contracts is recognized in accordance with IAS 11 Construction Contracts with the use of the percentage-of-completion method – provided that the conditions for application are fulfilled. The percentage of completion is mainly calculated on the basis of the ratio on the balance sheet date of the output volume already delivered to the total output volume to be delivered. The percentage of completion is also calculated from the ratio of the actual costs already incurred on the balance sheet date to the planned total costs (cost-to-cost method). If the results of construction contracts cannot be reliably estimated, revenue is calculated using the zero profit method in the amount of the costs incurred and probably recoverable.

Revenue from the provision of services is recognized in accordance with IAS 18.20 with the use of the percentage of completion method – provided that the conditions for application are fulfilled. In the area of services, percentage of completion is mainly calculated using the cost-to-cost method.

Revenue from the sale of goods is recognized according to the criteria of IAS 18.14 (revenue recognition on the transfer of significant risks and rewards of ownership).

In the context of concession projects, construction services provided are recognized as revenue in accordance with IAS 11 using the percentage of completion method.

In the operating phase of concession projects, the recognition of revenue from operating services depends upon whether a financial or an intangible asset is to be received as consideration for the construction services provided.

续表

然而，某些合同可能包括由特许权授予方做出的仅涵盖部分投资的付款承诺，而剩余金额由向使用者收取的特许权使用费涵盖。 在这种情况下，在金融资产模式下确认特许权授予方担保的投资金额，在无形资产模式下确认剩余金额。

表 33. 2——IFRIC 12、会计政策、SIC 29、各种特许服务权安排的披露

Bilfinger Berger SE——年报——2011 年 12 月 31 日

6. 重大会计政策(摘要)

建造合同的收入根据《国际会计准则第 11 号——建造合同》采用完工百分比法进行确认——前提是应用条件得到满足。完工百分比的计算主要是基于资产负债表日已经交付的产出量占需交付的总产出量的比率。此外,完工百分比还可根据资产负债表日已经发生的实际成本占计划总成本的比率(成本对成本法)。如果不能可靠估计建造合同的结果,收入采用零利润法按照已经发生并可能回收的成本计算。

提供服务的收入根据 IAS 18 第 20 段采用完工百分比法进行确认——前提是应用条件得到满足。在服务领域,主要采用成本对成本法计算完工百分比。

销货收入根据 IAS 18 第 14 段中的标准进行确认(在所有权相关的重大风险和报酬转移时确认收入)。

在特许权项目的情况下,所提供的建造服务根据 IAS 11 采用完工百分比法确认为收入。

在特许权项目的经营阶段,来自经营服务的收入确认取决于所提供建造服务的对价是以金融资产或无形资产的方式收取。

Con.

If a financial asset is to be recognized, i. e. the operator receives a fixed payment from the grantor irrespective of the extent of use, revenue from the provision of operator services is recognized according to IAS 18 using the percentage of completion method. The percentage of completion is calculated using the cost-to-cost method.

If an intangible asset is to be recognized, that is, the operator receives payments from the users or from the client depending on use, the payments for use are recognized as revenue according to IAS 18 generally in line with the extent of use of the infrastructure by the users.

If the operator receives both use - dependent and use - independent payments, revenue recognition is split in accordance with the ratio of the two types of payment.

18. Receivables from concession projects

Receivables from concession projects represent all services provided in connection with the construction of public - private - partnership (PPP) projects for which fixed payments have been agreed irrespective of the extent of use. Due to the length of the payment plans, receivables are measured at the present value of amortized cost. The annual accumulation of interest on these discounted amounts is presented as interest income under other operating income. Gtrantors' payments are divided into a portion to be deducted from the receivables and a portion for the regular concession services.

Funds received in the context of loan financing but not yet applied are also presented.

The capitalized amounts from concession projects have corresponding items in non-recourse liabilities. These amounts are presented under financial debt, thereof € 338.7 million as non-current (2010: € 1,624.1 million) and € 8.7 million as current (2010: € 19.3 million).

Receivables from concession projects are comprised as follows (€ million):

	2011	2010
Receivables from concession projects	372.4	1,782.7
Receivables from project - financing funds not yet applied	4.6	5.8
	377.0	**1,788.5**
Non-recourse financial liabilities	**347.4**	**1,643.4**

Receivables decreased by € 1,504.9 million and non-recourse financial debt decreased by € 1,415.0 million due to the classification of 10 fully consolidated projects as a disposal group.

续表

如果确认一项金融资产，即无论使用程度，经营方从授予方处收取固定的款项，则来自提供经营服务的收入根据 IAS 18 采用完工百分比法进行确认。完工百分比采用成本对成本法计算。

如果确认一项无形资产，即根据使用情况，经营方从使用者或客户处收取款项，则使用款项根据 IAS 18 通常按照使用者对基础设施的使用程度确认为收入。

如果经营方既取得依据使用情况的款项又取得不依据使用情况的款项，则收入根据两种付款类型的比率分别确认。

18. 来自特许权项目的应收款项

来自特许权项目的应收款项代表与公私合作关系（public - private - partnership）项目的建造相关的所有服务，就这些服务已约定无论使用程度的固定款项。由于付款计划的时间跨度，应收款项以摊余成本的现值计量。这些折现金额的年度累计利息在其他营业收入中列报为利息收入。授予方的付款一部分从应收款项中扣除，一部分作为常规特许服务的对价。

在贷款融资的情况下，已收到但尚未申用的资金也要列报。

来自特许权项目的资本化金额在无追索权负债中有对应的项目。这些金额在财务负债中列报，其中 3.387 亿欧元为非流动负债（2010 年：16.241 亿欧元），870 万欧元为流动负债（2010 年：1,930 万欧元）。

来自特许权项目的应收款项构成如下（百万欧元）：

	2011	2010
来自特许权项目的应收款项	372.4	1,782.7
来自项目的应收款项——尚未申用的融资资金	4.6	5.8
	377.0	**1,788.5**
无追索权金融负债	**347.4**	**1,643.4**

由于 10 个完全合并的项目被分类为处置组，应收款项减少 15.049 亿欧元，无追索权金融负债减少 14.150 亿欧元。

Table 33.3 – SIC 29, disclosure of various service concessions arrangements

Bilfinger Berger AG – Annual report – 31 December 2011

The most important fully consolidated concession projects are:

	Investment volume € million	**Bilfinger Berger's share of project in %**	**Project status**	**Period of concession**
Transport infrastructure				
M1 Westlink, United Kingdom	230	75	In operation	2009 – 2036
Golden Ears Bridge, Canada	800	100	In operation	2009 – 2041
Northeast Stoney Trail, Canada	293	100	In operation	2009 – 2039
Building construction				
Bedford Schools, United Kingdom	41	100	In operation	2006 – 2035
Victoria Prisons, Australia	150	100	In operation	2006 – 2031
District Administration Center Unna, Germany	24	90	In operation	2006 – 2031
Coventry Schools, United Kingdom	36	100	In operation	2007 – 2035
Royal Women's Hospital, Australia	198	100	In operation	2008 – 2033
Burg Correctional Facility, Germany	100	90	In operation	2009 – 2034
Borders Schools, United Kingdom	137	75	In operation	2009 – 2038
Clackmannanshire Schools, United Kingdom	136	85	In operation	2009 – 2039
Staffordshire Fire Stations, United Kingdom	54	85	Under construction	2011 – 2036
Women's College Hospital, Canada	350	100	Under construction	2015 – 2045

表 33.3——SIC 29、各种特许服务权安排的披露

Bilfinger Berger AG—年报—2011 年 12 月 31 日

最为重要的完全合并的特许权项目为：

	Bilfinger Berger 投资金额 百万欧元	所占份额 占%	项目状态	特许权期限
运输设施				
M1Westlink，英国	230	75	运营中	2009—2036 年
Golden Ears Bridge，加拿大	800	100	运营中	2009—2041 年
Northeast Stoney Trail，加拿大	293	100	运营中	2009—2039 年
建筑物建造				
Bedford 学校，英国	41	100	运营中	2006—2035 年
Victoria 监狱，澳大利亚	150	100	运营中	2006—2031 年
Unna 地区行政中心，德国	24	90	运营中	2006—2031 年
Coventry 学校，英国	36	100	运营中	2007—2035 年
皇家妇女医院，澳大利亚	198	100	运营中	2008—2033 年
Burg 监狱，德国	100	90	运营中	2009—2034 年
Borders 学校，英国	137	75	运营中	2009—2038 年
Clackmannanshire 学校，英国	136	85	运营中	2009—2039 年
Staffordshire 消防站，英国	54	85	建造中	2011—2036 年
女子学院医院，加拿大	350	100	建造中	2015—2045 年

Con.

The transport infrastructure concession projects are for highways, including bridges and tunnels. The building concession projects are for schools, hospitals, prisons, public – sector administrative buildings and fire stations. Concession fees are dependent on the availability of the transport infrastructure or building, are paid by the concession client and are inflation indexed. The concession agreements are design-build-finance-operate contracts and also include the obligation to perform maintenance and major repairs. At the end of the concession period, the transport infrastructures and buildings are transferred to the concession client. There are generally no extension or termination options.

Table 33.4 – Disclosure relating to concession intangible assets

Veolia Environnement SA – Annual Report – 31 December 2011

6 Concession intangible assets

Movements in the net carrying amount of concession intangible assets during 2011are as follows:

(€ millions)	**As of December 31, 2010**	Additions	Disposals	Impairment losses	Amortization	Changes in consolidation scope	Foreign exchange translation	Transfers to Assets classifiedas held for sale	Other	**As of December 31, 2011**
Concession intangible assets, gross	**5,851.0**	620.7	(51.3)	–	–	(28.7)	167.5	272.0	(26.6)	**6,804.6**
Amortization & impairment losses	**(1,686.4)**	–	39.7	(146.3)	(292.6)	6.4	(20.4)	(116.8)	40.9	**(2,175.5)**
Concession intangible assets, net	**4,164.6**	**620.7**	**(11.6)**	**(146.3)**	**(292.6)**	**(22.3)**	**147.1**	**155.2**	**14.3**	**4,629.1**

Additions concern the Water division in the amount of €315.8 million, the Energy Services Division in the amount of € 146.9 million and the Environmental Services division in the amount of €127.4 million.

A breakdown of **impairment losses** recognized in 2011 is presented in Note 20. These mainly concerned:

- the Environmental Services division in Italy (€91.1 million) and France (€12.1 million);
- the Water division in Italy (€22.6 million);
- the Energy Services division in France (€13.2 million).

续表

运输基础设施特许权项目内容为高速路，包括桥梁和隧道。建筑物特许权项目内容包括学校、医院、监狱、公共部门行政大楼及消防站。特许权费用取决于运输基础设施或建筑物的可用性，由特许权客户支付，并与通货膨胀指数挂钩。这些特许权协议为设计－建造－融资－运营合同，也包括执行维护和大修的义务。在特许权期末，运输基础设施和建筑物移交给特许权客户。一般没有延期或终止的选择权。

表 33.4——与特许权无形资产相关的披露

Veolia 环境 SA——年报——2011 年 12 月 31 日

6 特许权无形资产

2011 年期间特许权无形资产账面净值的变动如下：

（百万欧元）	于 2010 年 12 月 31 日	增加	处置	减值损失	摊销	合并范围变化	外币折算	转至持有待售资产	其他	于 2011 年 12 月 31 日
特许权无形资产毛值	**5,851.0**	620.7	(51.3)	–	–	(28.7)	167.5	272.0	(26.6)	**6,804.6**
摊销和减值损失	**(1,686.4)**	–	39.7	(146.3)	(292.6)	6.4	(20.4)	(116.8)	40.9	**(2,175.5)**
特许权无形资产净值	**4,164.6**	**620.7**	**(11.6)**	**(146.3)**	**(292.6)**	**(22.3)**	**147.1**	**155.2**	**14.3**	**4,629.1**

增加额涉及水资源部门增加 3.158 亿欧元，能源服务部门增加 1.469 亿欧元以及环境服务部门增加 1.274 亿欧元。

2011 年确认的**减值损失**明细在附注 20 中列报。这些主要涉及：

- 意大利的环境服务部门（9,110 万欧元）和法国的环境服务部门（1,210 万欧元）；
- 意大利的水资源部门（2,260 万欧元）；
- 法国的能源服务部门（1,320 万欧元）。

Con.

Foreign exchange translation gains and losses are primarily due to the appreciation of the Chinese renminbi yuan against the euro in the amount of € 134.9 million.

Transfers to Assets classified as held for sale mainly concern the reclassification out of 'Assets classified as held for sale' of the assets of Water division activities in Gabon (+€ 175.8 million) following the decision to interrupt the divestiture process and the assets of the Veolia Transdev group reclassified as discontinued operation (−€ 13.2 million, see Note 4).

Concession intangible assets break down by division as follows:

As of December 31, 2011

(€ million)	Gross carrying amount	Amortization and impairment losses	Net carrying amount	**As of December 31, 2010**	**As of December 31, 2009**
Water	4,903.0	(1,335.3)	**3,567.7**	3,196.8	2,844.8
Enviromental Services	759.4	(361.0)	**398.4**	385.5	263.2
Energy Services	1,046.9	(453.1)	**593.8**	513.1	480.0
Transportation	–	–	–	14.4	–
Other	95.3	(26.1)	**69.2**	54.8	36.8
Concessions intangible assets	**6,804.6**	**(2,175.5)**	**4,629.1**	**4,164.6**	**3,624.8**

Recap: Movements in the net carrying amount of concession intangible assets during **2010** are as follows:

(€ million)	**As of December 31, 2009**	Additions	Disposals	Impairment losses	Amortization/ reversals	Changes in consolidation scope	Foreign exchange translation	Transfers to Assets classified as held for sale	Other	**As of December 31, 2010**
Concession intangible assets, gross	5,129.1	497.4	(17.3)	–	–	223.8	193.9	(302.9)	127.0	5,851.0
Amortization and impairment losses	(1,504.3)	–	11.0	(6.5)	(256.6)	(35.8)	(16.8)	123.3	(0.7)	(1,686.4)
CONCESSION INTANGIBLE ASSETS, NET	**3,624.8**	**497.4**	**(6.3)**	**(6.5)**	**(256.6)**	**188.0**	**177.1**	**(179.6)**	**126.3**	**4,164.6**

Additions concern the Water division in the amount of € 339.0 million, the Energy Services division in the amount of € 71.8 million and the Environmental Services division in the amount of € 53.5 million.

续表

外币折算损益主要是由于人民币对欧元升值而产生，金额为 1.349 亿欧元。

转至持有待售资产主要涉及在作出中断分拆进程的决策后，将加蓬水资源部门业务活动的资产（1.758 亿欧元）从“持有待售资产”转出，以及将 Veolia Transdev 集团的资产重分类为终止经营（ －1,320 万欧元，见附注 4）。

特许权无形资产按部门的明细如下：

于 2011 年 12 月 31 日

（百万欧元）	账面毛值	摊销和减值损失	账面净值	**于 2010 年 12 月 31 日**	**于 2009 年 12 月 31 日**
水资源	4,903.0	(1,335.3)	**3,567.7**	3,196.8	2,844.8
环境服务	759.4	(361.0)	**398.4**	385.5	263.2
能源服务	1046.9	(453.1)	**593.8**	513.1	480.0
运输	–	–	–	14.4	–
其他	95.3	(26.1)	**69.2**	54.8	36.8
特许权无形资产	**6,804.6**	**(2,175.5)**	**4,629.1**	**4,164.6**	**3,624.8**

回顾：**2010** 年期间特许权无形资产账面净值的变动如下：

（百万欧元）	**于 2009 年 12 月 31 日**	增加	处置减值损失		摊销/冲回	合并范围变化	外币折算	转至持有待售资产	其他	**于 2010 年 12 月 31 日**
特许权无形资产毛值	5,129.1	497.4	(17.3)	–	–	223.8	193.9	(302.9)	127.0	5,851.0
摊销和减值损失	(1,504.3)	–	11.0	(6.5)	(256.6)	(35.8)	(16.8)	123.3	(0.7)	(1,686.4)
特许权无形资产净值	**3,624.8**	**497.4**	**(6.3)**	**(6.5)**	**(256.6)**	**188.0**	**177.1**	**(179.6)**	**126.3**	**4,164.6**

增加额涉及水资源部门增加 3.39 亿欧元，能源服务部门增加 7,180 万欧元以及环境服务部门增加 5,350 万欧元。

Con.

Changes in consolidation scope mainly concern external growth transactions in the Water division with the acquisition of certain United Utilities Group businesses in the amount of €101.8 million and the unwinding of companies previously held jointly with Suez Environnement in the amount of €50.6 million.

Foreign exchange translation gains and losses are primarily due to the appreciation of the Chinese renminbi yuan against the euro in the amount of €158.3 million.

Table 33.5 – Disclosure relating to financial asset

Veolia Environnement SA – Annual Report – 31 December 2011

11 Non–current and current operating financial assets

Operating financial assets comprise financial assets resulting from the application of IFRIC 12 on accounting for concession arrangements and from the application of IFRIC 4 (see Notes 1.20 and 1.21).

Movements in the net carrying amount of non–current and current operating financial assets during **2011** are as follows:

(€ millions)	**As of December 31, 2010**	New financial assets	Repay-ments/ disposals	Impair-ment losses (1)	changes in consoli-dation scope	Foreign exchange trans-lation	Non-current/ current reclassi-fication	Transfer to Assets classified as held for sale	Other	**As of December 31, 2011**
Gross	5,317.3	381.0	(36.9)	–	(64.7)	33.3	(406.6)	(135.2)	48.3	5,136.5
Impairment losses	(62.0)	–	–	(4.3)	–	(0.1)	5.0	–	13.2	(48.2)
Non-current operating financial assets	**5,255.3**	**381.0**	**(36.9)**	**(4.3)**	**(64.7)**	**33.2**	**(401.6)**	**(135.2)**	**61.5**	**5,088.3**
Gross	373.3	0.2	(404.1)	–	(9.3)	2.0	406.6	(24.9)	13.2	357.0
Impairement losses	–	–	–	5.0	–	–	(5.0)	–	–	–
Current operating financial assets	**373.3**	**0.2**	**(404.1)**	**5.0**	**(9.3)**	**2.0**	**401.6**	**(24.9)**	**13.2**	**357.0**
Non-current and current operating financial assets	**5,628.6**	**381.2**	**(441.0)**	**0.7**	**(74.0)**	**35.2**	–	**(160.1)**	**74.7**	**5,445.3**

续表

合并范围变化主要涉及水资源部门的外部成长交易——以1.018亿欧元的金额收购了联合公用事业集团的某些业务；以5,060万欧元的金额处置了之前与苏伊士环境公司共同持有的公司。

外币折算损益主要是由于人民币对欧元升值而产生，金额为1.583亿欧元。

表33.5——与金融资产相关的披露

Veolia环境SA——年报——2011年12月31日

11 非流动和流动经营性金融资产

经营性金融资产包含对特许权安排应用IFRIC 12进行会计处理以及应用IFRIC 4所产生的金融资产（见附注1.20和附注1.21）。

2011年非流动和流动经营性金融资产账面净值的变动如下：

（百万欧元）	于2010年12月31日	新增金融资产	收款/处置	减值损失(1)	合并范围的变更	外币折算	非流动/流动重分类	转至持有待售资产	其他	于2011年12月31日
毛值	5,317.3	381.0	(36.9)	–	(64.7)	33.3	(406.6)	(135.2)	48.3	5,136.5
减值损失	(62.0)	–	–	(4.3)	–	(0.1)	5.0	–	13.2	(48.2)
非流动经营性金融资产	**5,255.3**	**381.0**	**(36.9)**	**(4.3)**	**(64.7)**	**33.2**	**(401.6)**	**(135.2)**	**61.5**	**5,088.3**
毛值	373.3	0.2	(404.1)	–	(9.3)	2.0	406.6	(24.9)	13.2	357.0
减值损失	–	–	–	5.0	–	–	(5.0)	–	–	–
流动经营性金融资产	**373.3**	**0.2**	**(404.1)**	**5.0**	**(9.3)**	**2.0**	**401.6**	**(24.9)**	**13.2**	**357.0**
非流动和流动经营性金融资产	**5,628.6**	**381.2**	**(441.0)**	**0.7**	**(74.0)**	**35.2**	**–**	**(160.1)**	**74.7**	**5,445.3**

Con.

(1) *Impairment losses are recorded in operating income.*

The principal **new operating financial assets** in 2011 mainly concern:

- the Water division and in particular projects in Berlin (€ 129 million);
- the Energy Services division and in particular cogeneration plants (€ 66.9 million);
- the Environmental Services division and in particular new Private Finance Initiative (PFI) contracts for the processing and disposal of residual waste in the United Kingdom (€ 47.4 million).

The principal **repayments and disposals of operating financial assets** in 2011 concern:

- the Water division and in particular projects in Berlin (–€ 141.3 million);
- the Energy Services division and in particular cogeneration plants (–€ 110.0 million);
- the Environmental Services division and in particular the non – recourse assignment of Valomed receivables to the Royal Bank of Scotland (–€ 28.5 million).

Foreign exchange translation gains and losses on current and non – current operating financial assets mainly concern the Water division (€ 20.8 million) and the Environmental Services division (€ 17.4 million), primarily due to the appreciation of the Chinese renminbi yuan and the pound sterling

Non-current/current reclassifications mainly concern:

- the Water division and in particular projects in Berlin (€ 140.8 million);
- the Energy Services division and in particular cogeneration plants (€ 85.4 million).

Changes in consolidation scope mainly concern the impacts of the Veolia Transdev combination(–€ 60.5 million, including –€ 52.5 million classified as non-current, see Note 4).

Transfers to Assets classified as held for sale mainly concern the assets of the Veolia Transdev group reclassified as discontinued operation(–€ 120.6 million, see Note 4) and the placing of Citelum in the Energy Services division for sale(–€ 46.7 million).

续表

(1) *减值损失记录于营业收入中。* 2011 年主要的**新增经营性金融资产**主要涉及： • 水资源部门，特别是在柏林的项目（1.29 亿欧元）； • 能源服务部门，特别是废热发电厂（6,690 万欧元）； • 环境服务部门，特别是为处理和处置英国的剩余废物的新的私营主动融资（Private Finance Initiative）合同（4,740 万欧元）。 2011 年主要的**经营性金融资产收款和处置**涉及： • 水资源部门，特别是在柏林的项目（－1.413 亿欧元）； • 能源服务部门，特别是废热发电厂（－1.100 亿欧元）； • 环境服务部门，特别是 Valomed 应收款项向苏格兰皇家银行的无追索权转让（－2,850 万欧元）。 流动和非流动经营性金融资产的**外币折算损益**主要涉及水资源部门（2,080 万欧元）和环境服务部门（1,740 万欧元），主要是由于人民币和英镑的升值。 **非流动/流动重分类**主要涉及： • 水资源部门，特别是在柏林的项目（1.408 亿欧元）； • 能源服务部门，特别是废热发电厂（8,540 万欧元）。 **合并范围变化**主要涉及 Veolia Transdev 合并的影响（－6,050 万欧元，包括分类为长期的－5,250 万欧元，参见附注 4）。 **转至持有待售资产**主要涉及 Veolia Transdev 集团的资产被重分类为非持续经营（－1.206 亿欧元，参见附注 4）以及准备出售能源服务部门的 Citelum（－4,670 万欧元）。

Effective date and transitional arrangements

33.129 IFRIC 12 is effective for annual periods beginning on or after 1 January 2008. Within the European Union, the interpretation is effective for accounting periods commencing on or after 29 March 2009.

33.130 In accordance with IAS 8, a change in accounting policy that is made on the initial application of IFRIC 12 should be made retrospectively. [IFRIC 12 para 29].

33.131 Consistent with IAS 8, IFRIC 12 provides relief from full retrospective application if it is impracticable for the operator to do so. This may be in circumstances where the service concession arrangements were entered into many years ago and detailed records about construction activities necessary to perform retrospective adjustments have not been retained. In those circumstances if, for any particular service concession arrangement, retrospective application to beginning of the earliest period for which figures are presented is impracticable, then the operator should:

- recognise financial assets and intangible assets that existed at the start of the earliest period presented;
- use the previous carrying amounts of those financial and intangible assets (however previously classified) as their carrying amounts as at that date; and
- test financial and intangible assets recognised at that date for impairment, unless this is not practicable, in which case the amounts should be tested for impairment as at the start of the current period.

[IFRIC 12 para 30].

33.132 The above transitional relief, which is available to existing users of IFRS and to first-time adopters, may appear to be relatively straight forward, but it is likely to create problems in practice. For instance, an operator that entered into a service concession arrangement many years ago may have recorded the infrastructure assets used for the provision of public service as its own property,

生效日期和过渡性安排

33.129 IFRIC 12 自 2008 年 1 月 1 日或以后日期开始的年度期间生效。在欧盟范围内，该解释公告自 2009 年 3 月 29 日或以后日期开始的会计期间生效。

33.130 根据 IAS 8，因初始采用 IFRIC 12 而进行的会计政策变更应当进行追溯调整。[IFRIC 12 第 29 段]。

33.131 与 IAS 8 相一致，如果经营方采用完全追溯调整法不切实可行，IFRIC 12 对此提供了豁免。这可能是如下的情况：特许服务权安排在多年前签署，而进行追溯调整所必不可少的建造活动详细记录未被保留。在那些情况下，如果对于任何特别的特许服务权安排，经营方在列报最早期间的期初进行追溯调整不切实可行，那么经营方应当：

- 确认在列报最早期间的期初存在的金融资产和无形资产；
- 使用那些金融资产和无形资产之前的账面金额（无论之前如何分类）作为该日的账面金额；以及
- 在该日对金融资产和无形资产进行减值测试，除非减值测试不切实可行，在该种情况下则在本期期初进行减值测试。

[IFRIC 12 第 30 段]。

33.132 上述可供国际财务报告准则的现有使用者和首次采用者使用的过渡性豁免很可能看起来相对简单，但在实务中可能产生问题。例如，一个在多年前签署特许服务权安排的经营方可能已根据之前的一般公认会计原则将用于提供公共服务的基础设施资产记录为自有不动产、工厂和设备。根据过渡性豁免条款，它可能需要将其基础设施资产的账面价值根据特许权安排的条

plant and equipment under previous GAAP. Under the transitional relief provisions it may need to reclassify the carrying value of its infrastructure assets either as intangible assets, financial assets or both depending on the terms of the concession arrangement. Reclassifying the carrying value from tangible to intangible asset is likely to be straightforward, although it may have to be tested for impairment as considered in the example below.

Example – Retrospective application is impracticable

An operator has been operating and maintaining a toll bridge for some years under a 30 year service concession arrangement. The operator receives tolls from users based on usage. There are no shortfall guarantees in place. As the operator bears all the demand risk, the construction cost of the bridge was classified as property, plant and equipment under previous GAAP and depreciated over the life of the concession period.

The service concession arrangement falls within IFRIC 12's scope, but the operator believes that retrospective application is impracticable because records are not available to reliably estimate the construction margin and, hence, the fair value of the construction services undertaken during the concession period.

In this situation, the operator will take advantage of the transitional relief provisions of IFRIC 12 by reclassifying the carrying value of property, plant and equipment as an intangible asset at the start of the earliest period presented. At that date, the operator would need to test the intangible asset for impairment in accordance with IAS 36. If impairment testing at the start of the earliest period presented is impracticable, it should be undertaken at the start of the current period.

33.133 However, problems may arise if the property, plant and equipment's carrying value is classified as a loan or receivable under IFRIC 12. In that situation, it is highly likely that the carrying value of the receivable, which is equal to the carrying value of the tangible asset at the time of the reclassification, would be different from what would have been its true carrying value had the concession arrangement been accounted for as a financial asset since inception. This is because

款重新分类为无形资产、金融资产或二者皆有。将账面价值从有形资产重新分类为无形资产很可能是简单的，尽管可能不得不进行减值测试，如下述示例中所考虑的。

示例——追溯调整不切实可行

根据一项为期 30 年的特许服务权安排，经营方已经运营和维护一座收费桥梁多年。经营方基于使用情况向使用者收取通行费。这里没有差额担保。由于经营方承担全部需求风险，根据之前的一般公认会计原则，桥梁的建造成本被分类为不动产、工厂和设备，并在特许权期间内进行折旧。

特许服务权安排属于 IFRIC 12 的范围，但经营方相信追溯调整是不切实可行的，因为没有记录来可靠估计建造毛利，因此无法估计在特许权期间内所从事的建造服务的公允价值。

在这一情况下，经营方将利用 IFRIC 12 的过渡性豁免条款，在列报最早期间的期初将不动产、工厂和设备的账面价值重新分类为无形资产。在该日，经营方将需要根据 IAS 36 对无形资产进行减值测试。如果在列报最早期间的期初进行减值测试是不切实可行的，则应该在本期期初进行。

33.133 然而，如果根据 IFRIC 12，不动产、工厂和设备的账面价值被分类为贷款或应收款项，则可能出现问题。在该情况下，该应收款项的账面价值（在重分类时等于有形资产账面价值）非常可能不同于它如果从特许权安排的开始就以金融资产核算的真实账面价值。这是因为在有形资产模式下，在 IFRIC 12 过渡日期之前特许权产生的全部现金流量会被确认为收入，而在金融资产模式下，一部分的现金流量会被用来减少根据实际利率法进行会计处

under a tangible asset model the entire cash flows from the concession prior to the date of transition to IFRIC 12 would have been recognised as revenue, whilst under a financial asset model a proportion of the cash flows would have been applied to reduce the amortised cost of the receivable accounted for under the effective interest method.

33. 134 The issue that arises in practice is the accounting for the receivable subsequent to date of transition, as it would be necessary to segment the cash flows arising during the remaining period of the arrangement between repayment of the receivable and recognition of service revenue. The interpretation provides no guidance on how this split should be carried out. It is likely that the operators would apply the relative fair value method of making the apportionment as discussed in paragraph 33. 64 above, but judgement is needed in determining an effective interest rate and an appropriate service margin. However, as the interpretation is silent, any reasonable method of allocating the future consideration receivable between capital and revenue would be acceptable.

33. 135 Further complications may arise if the operator is required to recognise an intangible as well as a financial asset. For instance, the terms of the toll bridge arrangement discussed in paragraph 33. 132 above may include a shortfall guarantee provided by the grantor. An arrangement of this type would lead to recognising a financial asset representing the minimum guaranteed amount and an intangible asset for sums collected from users in excess of the minimum. In this situation, the operator could again follow the relative fair value method in allocating the carrying value of the property, plant and equipment at transition date or, alternatively, estimate the fair value of the financial asset by discounting the future amounts payable under the guarantee and deducting this from the transition carrying amount of the property, plant and equipment to obtain the intangible component. Again, a considerable amount of judgement would be required in making a reliable apportionment so that the financial amounts reported in periods subsequent to date of transition are fairly representative of the economics of the concession arrangement. Adequate disclosures should be given to explain and supplement the allocation method adopted.

理的应收款项的摊余成本。

33.134　在实务中出现的问题是过渡日以后应收款项的会计处理，因为有必要将安排的剩余期间产生的现金流量在收回应收款项和确认服务收入之间进行划分。该解释公告未提供如何进行这一分割的指引。经营方可能如上述第 33.64 段中所述使用相对公允价值法进行分配，但是在确定实际利率和恰当的服务毛利时需要运用判断。然而，因为解释公告并未明确，所以任何在资本和收入间分配未来的应收对价的合理方法都是可以接受的。

33.135　如果要求经营方同时确认一项无形资产和一项金融资产，则可能会出现进一步的问题。例如，上述第 33.132 段中所探讨的收费桥梁安排的条款可能包括由授予方提供的差额担保。这一类安排将导致确认一项代表最低担保金额的金融资产和一项代表从使用者处收取超过最低金额的总数的无形资产。在这一情况下，经营方可以再次按照相对公允价值法在过渡日分配不动产、工厂和设备的账面价值，或者，也可通过对担保的未来应付金额进行折现以估计金融资产的公允价值，并从不动产、工厂和设备的过渡账面金额中扣除上述金额以获得无形资产部分。再次说明，在进行可靠的分配时需要运用大量的判断，以便使过渡日后续期间报告的财务数据能够公允代表特许权安排的经济实质。为了解释和补充所采用的分配方法，应当做出充分的披露。

Future developments

33.136 In 2011, the IFRS IC received a request to address an issue that is related to contractual payments, including variable payments, made by an operator under a service concession arrangement. The requestor asked in which circumstances those payments should be either (i) recognised at the start of the concession as an asset with a liability to make the related payments; or (ii) treated as executory in nature and recognised over the term of the concession arrangement. In May 2012, the committee discussed a draft amendment to IFRIC 12 to incorporate the principles that the IASB is developing in its leases project. The Committee tentatively agreed that the amendment should be published at the same time as a revised exposure draft on leases.

未来发展

33.136　在 2011 年，国际财务报告准则解释委员会收到一项处理一个与合同付款相关问题的请求，包括经营方根据特许服务权安排进行的可变付款。请求者询问在哪些情况下那些付款应（i）在特许权开始时确认为资产，并确认一项进行相关付款的负债；或（ii）在性质上处理为待执行性，并在特许权安排期间确认。2012 年 5 月，委员会讨论了 IFRIC 12 的修改草案，该草案体现了国际会计准则理事会正在其租赁项目中制定的原则。委员会暂时同意该修改应当与修订后的租赁征求意见稿同时发布。

PwC Assurance Service Contacts
联系普华永道审计业务部

北京 Beijing
梁伟坚 Thomas Leung
电话 Tel：+86（10）6533 2838
电子邮件 Email：thomas. w. leung@ cn. pwc. com

上海 Shanghai
李丹 Daniel Li
电话 Tel：+86（21）2323 3388
电子邮件 Email：daniel. li@ cn. pwc. com

重庆 Chongqing
李松波 Bobby Lee
电话 Tel：+86（23）6393 7388
电子邮件 Email：bobby. lee@ cn. pwc. com

深圳 Shenzhen
张展豪 Albert Cheung
电话 Tel：+86（755）8261 8833
电子邮件 Email：albert. cheung@ cn. pwc. com

大连 Dalian
关兆文 Dorman Kwan
电话 Tel：+86（411）8379 1666
电子邮件 Email：dorman. kwan@ cn. pwc. com

苏州 Suzhou
汪超 Arthur Wang
电话 Tel：+86（512）6273 1998
电子邮件 Email：arthur. wang@ cn. pwc. com

广州 Guangzhou
何国辉 Timothy Ho
电话 Tel：+86（20）3819 2888
电子邮件 Email：timothy. kf. ho@ hk. pwc. com

天津 Tianjin
郑广安 Kwong On Cheng
电话 Tel：+86（22）2318 3003
电子邮件 Email：kwong. on. cheng@ cn. pwc. com

青岛 Qingdao
张国俊 Kevin Zhang
电话 Tel：+86（532）8089 1818
电子邮件 Email：kevin. zhang@ cn. pwc. com

西安 Xi'an
叶骏 Joe Ye
电话 Tel：+86（29）8720 3998
电子邮件 Email：joe. ye@ cn. pwc. com

PwC Accounting Consulting Services Contacts
联系普华永道会计专业咨询服务

金以文 Yvonne Kam
电话 Tel：+86（21）2323 3267
电子邮件 Email：yvonne. kam@ cn. pwc. com

陈保郎 Baolang Chen
电话 Tel：+86（21）2323 2555
电子邮件 Email：baolang. chen@ cn. pwc. com

方毅贤 Ian Farrar
电话 Tel：+852 2289 2313
电子邮件 Email：ian. p. farrar@ hk. pwc. com

陈燕华 Tracy Chen
电话 Tel：+86（21）2323 3070
电子邮件 Email：tracy. yh. chen@ cn. pwc. com

许心莹 Samying Huie
电话 Tel：+86（10）6533 2965
电子邮件 Email：samying. s. huie@ cn. pwc. com

苏虹 Shelley So
电话 Tel：+852 2289 2955
电子邮件 Email：shelley. so@ hk. pwc. com

沈洁 Jie Shen
电话 Tel：+86（21）2323 3659
电子邮件 Email：jie. shen@ cn. pwc. com

陈嘉怡 Clarry Chan
电话 Tel：+852 2289 2169
电子邮件 Email：clarry. chan@ hk. pwc. com

阮慧瑶 Elza Yuen
电话 Tel：+852 2289 2314
电子邮件 Email：elza. yuen@ hk. pwc. com

戴奈尔 Nigel Dealy
电话 Tel：+852 2289 1221
电子邮件 Email：nigel. dd. dealy@ hk. pwc. com

白鸿安 Hendry Pai
电话 Tel：+86（10）6533 7760
电子邮件 Email：hendry. pai@ cn. pwc. com

吴慧莹 Monica Ng
电话 Tel：+852 2289 1218
电子邮件 Email：monica. wy. ng@ hk. pwc. com

梁少宝 Dorothy Leung
电话 Tel：+852 2289 2151
电子邮件 Email：dorothy. sp. leung@ hk. pwc. com

孙宇辉 Yuhui Sun
电话 Tel：+86（10）6533 7331
电子邮件 Email：yuhui. sun@ cn. pwc. com

For further help，please contact：
如需更多帮助，请联系：

北京 Beijing
中国北京市
朝阳区东三环中路 7 号
北京财富中心写字楼 A 座 26 楼
邮政编码 100020
26/F Office Tower A
Beijing Fortune Plaza
7 Dongsanhuan Zhong Road
Chaoyang District
Beijing 100020，PRC
电话 Tel：+86（10）6533 8888
传真 Fax：+86（10）6533 8800

重庆 Chongqing
中国重庆市渝中区邹容路 68 号
大都会商厦 19 楼 1905 室
邮政编码 400010
Room 1905
19/F Metropolitan Tower
68 Zou Rong Road
Chongqing 400010，PRC
电话 Tel：+86（23）6393 7888
传真 Fax：+86（23）6393 7200

大连 Dalian
中国大连市西岗区中山路 147 号
森茂大厦 8 楼
邮政编码 116011
8/F Senmao Building
147 Zhongshan Road
Xigang District
Dalian 116011，PRC
电话 Tel：+86（411）8379 1888
传真 Fax：+86（411）8379 1800

广州 Guangzhou
中国广州市天河区珠江新城
珠江西路 10 号
普华永道中心 18 楼
邮政编码 510623
18/F PwC Center
10 Zhujiang Xi Road
Pearl River New City
Tianhe District
Guangzhou 510623，PRC
电话 Tel：+86（20）3819 2000
传真 Fax：+86（20）3819 2100

杭州 Hangzhou
中国杭州市下城区环城北路208号
坤和中心3205室
邮政编码310006
Room 3205, Canhigh Center
208 Huancheng Road North
Xiacheng District
Hangzhou 310006, PRC
电话：+86（571）2807 6388
传真：+86（571）2807 6300

宁波 Ningbo
中国宁波市江东区民安东路268号
宁波国际金融服务中心E座1203室
邮政编码315040
Room 1203, Tower E
Ningbo International Financial Center
268 Min An Road East
Jiangdong District
Ningbo 315040, PRC
电话 Tel：+86（574）8187 1788
传真 Fax：+86（574）8187 1700

香港 Hong Kong
中国香港中环太子大厦22楼
22/F Prince's Building
Central
Hong Kong, PRC
电话 Tel：+852 2289 8888
传真 Fax：+852 2810 9888

青岛 Qingdao
中国青岛市市南区延安三路234号
海航万邦中心1号楼37楼
邮政编码266071
37/F Tower One, HNA IMC Center
234 Yanan Third Road, Shinan District
Qingdao 266071, PRC
电话 Tel：+86（532）8089 1888
传真 Fax：+86（532）8089 1800

澳门 Macau
中国澳门苏亚利斯博士大马路323号
中国银行大厦29楼
29/F Bank of China Building
323 Avenida Doutor Mario Soares
Macau, PRC
电话 Tel：+853 8799 5111
传真 Fax：+853 8799 5222

上海 Shanghai
中国上海市黄浦区湖滨路202号
企业天地2号楼
普华永道中心11楼
邮政编码200021
11/F PwC Center
2 Corporate Avenue
202 Hu Bin Road
Huangpu District
Shanghai 200021, PRC
电话 Tel：+86（21）2323 8888
传真 Fax：+86（21）2323 8800

南京 Nanjing
中国南京市鼓楼区中央路201号
南京国际广场南塔12A层01室
邮政编码210009
Room 12A01, South Tower
Nanjing International Center
201 Zhongyang Road
Gulou District
Nanjing 210009, PRC
电话 Tel：+86（25）6608 6288
传真 Fax：+86（25）6608 6210

深圳 Shenzhen
中国深圳市罗湖区深南东路5016号
京基100 － A座34楼
邮政编码518001
34/F Tower A, Kingkey 100
5016 Shennan East Road
Luohu District
Shenzhen 518001, PRC
电话 Tel：+86（755）8261 8888
传真 Fax：+86（755）8261 8800

新加坡 Singapore
新加坡 048424 邮区
PWC 大厦
克罗士街 8 号 17 楼
8 Cross Street # 17 – 00
PWC Building
Singapore 048424
电话 Tel：+65 6236 3388
传真 Fax：+65 6236 3300

天津 Tianjin
中国天津市和平区
南京路 189 号
津汇广场 2 座 36 楼
邮政编码 300051
36/F The Exchange Tower Two
189 Nanjing Road
Heping District
Tianjin 300051, PRC
电话 Tel：+86 (22) 2318 3333
传真 Fax：+86 (22) 2318 3300

苏州 Suzhou
中国苏州市苏州工业园区
旺墩路 188 号建屋大厦 1501 室
邮政编码 215028
Room 1501, Genway Tower
188 Wang Dun Road
Suzhou Industrial Park
Suzhou 215028, PRC
电话 Tel：+86 (512) 6273 1888
传真 Fax：+86 (512) 6273 1800

厦门 Xiamen
中国厦门市思明区鹭江道 8 号
国际银行大厦 11 楼 B 室
邮政编码 361001
Unit B, 11/F
International Plaza
8 Lujiang Road
Siming District
Xiamen 361001, PRC
电话 Tel：+86 (592) 210 7888
传真 Fax：+86 (592) 210 8800

台湾 Taiwan
中国台北市信义区 110
基隆路一段 333 号 27 楼
International Trade Building
27F, 333 Keelung Road, Section 1
Taipei 110, Taiwan
电话 Tel：+886 2 2729 6666
传真 Fax：+886 2 2757 6371

西安 Xi'an
中国西安市南关正街 88 号
长安国际中心 D 座 7 楼
邮政编码 710068
7/F, D Block, Chang'an Metropolis Center
88 Nanguan Street
Xi'an 710068, PRC
电话 Tel：+86 (29) 8469 2688
传真 Fax：+86 (29) 8469 2600

如欲了解更多资讯，敬请登陆公司网站：
For more information, please visit our websites at：
pwccn. com
pwchk. com

图书在版编目（CIP）数据

国际财务报告准则实务指引．第33章，特许服务权安排：汉英对照/谢智政等编译．—北京：中国财政经济出版社，2013.4
（普华永道国际财务报告准则实务指引系列）
ISBN 978-7-5095-4434-1

Ⅰ.①国… Ⅱ.①谢… Ⅲ.①会计准则-世界-汉、英 Ⅳ.①F233.1

中国版本图书馆CIP数据核字（2013）第076706号

责任编辑：吴　敏　　　　责任校对：杨瑞琦

中国财政经济出版社出版

URL：http：//www.cfeph.cn
E-mail：cfeph@cfeph.cn

社址：北京市海淀区阜成路甲28号　邮政编码：100142
营销中心电话：88190406　北京财经书店电话：64033436　84041336
北京富生印刷厂印刷　各地新华书店经销
787×1092毫米　16开　12.75印张　220 000字
2013年11月第1版　2013年11月北京第1次印刷
定价：33.00元
ISBN 978-7-5095-4434-1/F·3592
（图书出现印装问题，本社负责调换）
本社质量投诉电话：010-88190744
反盗版举报热线：88190492、88190446